4th Revised Edition

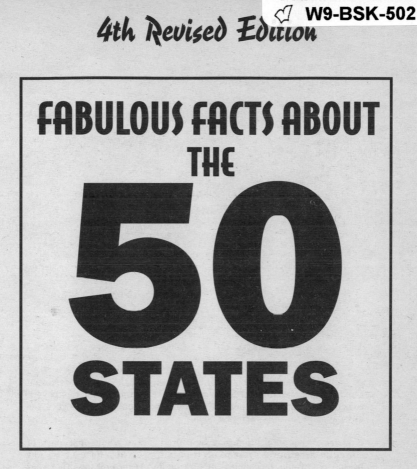

FABULOUS FACTS ABOUT THE 50 STATES

Wilma S. Ross

Scholastic Inc.
New York   Toronto   London   Auckland   Sydney

ISBN 0-590-44886-2

Text copyright © 1997, 1991, 1986, 1981, 1976, by Wilma Ross.
Illustrations copyright © 1986, 1981, 1976, by Scholastic Inc.
All rights reserved. Published by Scholastic Inc.

12 11 10 9 8 7 6 5 4 3 2   7 8 9/9 0 1 2/0

Printed in the U.S.A.

40

Contents

Before you visit any place listed in this book,
try to find out when it is scheduled to be open.

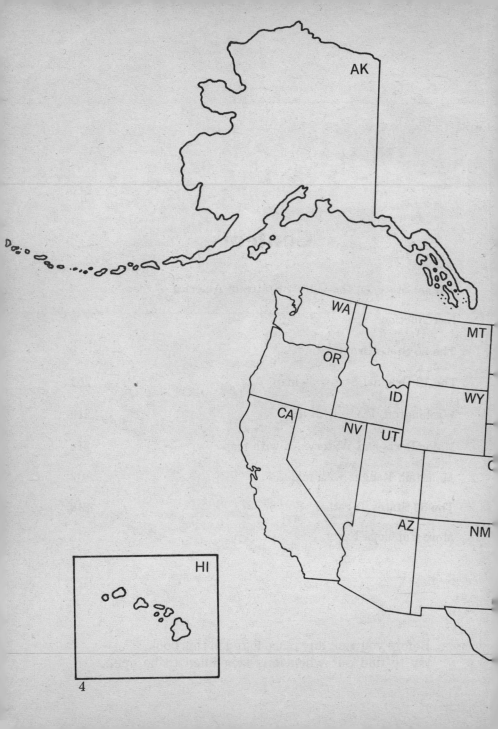

AK

WA

MT

OR

ID

WY

CA

NV

UT

C

AZ

NM

HI

4

The 50 States
of the
United States of America

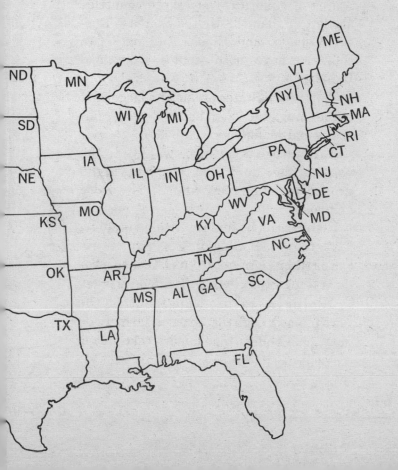

The 50 states together form the United States of America. Only three countries are larger than the United States — Russia, Canada, and China. And only two countries have more people — China and India.

The United States produces a large part of the things the world needs — food, minerals, and manufactured goods.

Agriculture is the name we give to the work farmers do. They grow plants in the ground and in greenhouses. They raise animals.

Fishing can be fun. But fishing is a business too — and a big one.

Together, agriculture and fishing produce things that become the food we eat.

Mining is taking things out of the earth. Not things that grow — farmers do that. The things that miners take out of the earth are oil and iron and other minerals. And some minerals come from the sea.

Manufacturing is making things. Building a car or ship or airplane is manufacturing. So is making milk into cheese, ice cream, or dried milk. Making wheat into flour or flour into bread is manufacturing too. Canning or freezing foods or cutting meat animals up to be packed for market — anything that is done to make a product into a different product — is manufacturing.

Records are kept that show how much money each kind of product adds to the total income of a state — after costs such as materials, supplies, and fuel have been paid. The products that bring in the most money are considered to be the most important.

Resident population
figures are from
the U.S. Census Estimates,
July 1, 1996.

Alabama AL

22nd State / December 14, 1819

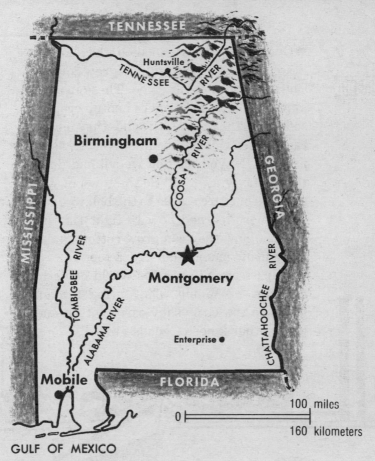

GULF OF MEXICO

POPULATION 4,273,000
AREA 52,423 square miles
     135,775 square kilometers
FLOWER Camellia
TREE Southern pine
BIRD Yellowhammer

9

◆Once Alabama was called the Cotton State. Almost all the farmers grew cotton. Then the boll weevils came. These insects killed the cotton. Farmers had no crop to sell. But the farmers found they could raise other things, such as livestock and peanuts. Maybe the boll weevil had done them a favor after all! So the town of Enterprise put up a statue to the boll weevil.

Farmers learned how to fight this insect. So now they can grow cotton again. They grow many other crops too.

Ships from all over the world come to the Port of Mobile. They bring foreign goods to the U.S. They carry cotton and many other kinds of goods away.

You will want to visit the Alabama Space and Rocket Center in Huntsville. That's where they figured out how to make the rocket that carried man to the moon. At the Center you can see and touch capsules brought back from space. You can fire a rocket engine. You can ride in a gyro chair and talk to a computer.

Other things to see:

Army Aviation Museum — at Fort Rucker

Birmingham Zoo — largest in Alabama

George Washington Carver Museum — at Tuskegee

Ivy Green — birthplace of Helen Keller, in Tuscumbia

USS *Alabama* — World War II battleship, in Mobile Bay

Main Products

Agriculture: cattle, chickens, cotton, dairy, eggs, fruit, hogs, peanuts, plants, soybeans, vegetables, wheat, wood. More than half the state is covered with forests.

Fishing: catfish, croakers, mullet, oysters, red snapper, shrimp. Pleasure fishing for large mouth bass, crappie, and sunfish brings Alabama even more money than commercial fishing earns.

Mining: bauxite, clay, coal, natural gas, petroleum, sand and gravel, shale, stone.

Manufacturing: chemicals, clothing, electronic equipment, food processing, furniture and fixtures, lumber and wood products, metals and metal products, paper products, rubber and plastic products, textiles, transportation equipment. Alabama coal and limestone are used to make pig iron and steel. Cloth and clothing are made from Alabama cotton. Furniture and paper are made from Alabama wood.

Alaska AK

49th State / January 3, 1959

RUSSIA

ARCTIC OCEAN

PT. BARROW

BERING STRAIT

BERING SEA

N

RIVER

YUKON

Mt. McKinley

Fairbanks

KUSKOKWIM RIVER

Anchorage

CANADA

PRIBILOF ISLANDS

Juneau

KODIAK ISLAND

PACIFIC OCEAN

```
0        300  miles
         480  kilometers
```

POPULATION 607,000
AREA 656,424 square miles
        1,700,139 square kilometers
FLOWER Forget-me-not
TREE Sitka spruce
BIRD Willow ptarmigan

◆The U.S. bought Alaska from Russia about 100 years ago. The U.S. paid less than two cents an acre. One Alaskan island is only two miles (about three kilometers) from a Russian island. The nearest state is Washington, 500 miles (800 kilometers) away.

Alaska is more than twice as big as Texas. It has many different kinds of weather. Around Fairbanks the temperature has gone as low as 70° below zero Fahrenheit (57° below zero Celsius). It has also gone as high as 100° above zero Fahrenheit (38° above zero Celsius).

Alaska has a longer coastline than all the other states together. The ocean water is full of sea life. Alaska's fish catch is one of the biggest of all the states. More than half of Alaska's land is still owned by the U.S. government — not by people or businesses.

The most northern spot in the U.S. is Point Barrow.

Alaska — the biggest state — has the fewest people per square mile. Towns are far apart. Long roads cost a lot to build in such wild country. So there aren't very many roads. Many people use planes to travel in the state. Others travel in boats along the coast. Rivers freeze in winter, but boats travel on them after the ice melts.

Fishermen and skiers and people who like beautiful country all visit Alaska. Mt. McKinley, the highest mountain in the U.S., is there. And some people get to see moose, elk, caribou, bears, and mountain goats.

Other things to see:

Dog-sled races — November to March, in many towns

Fur seals — in summer on the Pribilof Islands

Glacier Bay National Park — where 17 glaciers meet the water, near Juneau

Totem poles — near Ketchikan, and at Sitka National Historical Park, near Sitka

Main Products

Agriculture: barley, beef cattle, greenhouse and nursery products, hay, milk, oats, vegetables, wood. The growing season is short, but the sun shines 20 hours a day in summer. Things grow fast and big. A cabbage can weigh 80 pounds (about 36 kilograms).

Fishing: crabs, halibut, salmon, sea herring, shrimp. Alaska is first in fishing.

Mining: coal, gold, lead, natural gas, petroleum, sand and gravel, silver, stone, zinc. People are looking for more oil and other minerals in this huge state.

Manufacturing: food processing, lumber and wood products, petroleum and coal products, rocket and payload products.

The armed forces and visitors are both big businesses in Alaska.

Arizona AZ

48th State / February 14, 1912

FOUR CORNERS

UTAH

NEVADA

COLORADO RIVER

PAINTED DESERT

Grand Canyon

PETRIFIED FOREST

CALIFORNIA

NEW MEXICO

Phoenix ★

GILA RIVER

Tucson ●

N

0 ⊢——————⊣ 100 miles
160 kilometers

MEXICO

POPULATION 4,428,000
AREA 114,006 square miles
      295,276 square kilometers
FLOWER Saguaro cactus
TREE Paloverde
BIRD Cactus wren

17

◆About 800 years ago some Arizona Indians built canals to bring water to their fields. Then the water dried up, and the Indians moved away.

More than 100 years ago white settlers came to Phoenix. They found the old Indian irrigation canals. They hooked the canals up to a river and made the desert bloom again.

Arizona now has many dams. The dams store water for the crops. They make energy for homes and factories. They form lakes for people to enjoy.

Arizona has three national parks. It has 12 national monuments — more than any other state. When you visit, you will see Arizona's many natural and man-made wonders.

Other things to see:

Cactus — can be found at two national monuments and growing wild in the desert

Four Corners — only place in the U.S. where four states meet: Arizona, Colorado, New Mexico, and Utah

Ghost towns — at Tombstone and many other old mining towns

Grand Canyon National Park — world's largest canyon

Indian reservations — cover about a fourth of the state

Indian ruins — in many national monuments

Kitt Peak National Observatory — solar telescope on a 6,875-foot (2,063-meter) mountain

Oraibi — Indian village, in Hopi reservation, has been lived in longer than any other place in the U.S. — 800 years

Petrified Forest/Painted Desert National Park — logs turned to stone about 150 million years ago; sand of many different colors

San Xavier del Bac Mission — 1783 church, with carvings and paintings; near Tucson

Sunset Crater National Monument — cone and crater of a volcano

Main Products

Agriculture: beef cattle, cotton, fruit, hay, milk, sheep, vegetables, wheat. Arizona crops grow on irrigated land. Arizona farmers grow more cotton on an acre of land than any other U.S. farmers. Almost half the state is owned or run by the U.S. government. Cattle and sheep graze on government land.

Mining: coal, copper, gemstones, gold, molybdenum, sand and gravel, silver. More than half the copper in the U.S. is mined in Arizona. Gold, silver, molybdenum, and zinc are found with the copper. Arizona is first in molybdenum.

Manufacturing: chemicals; electric and electronic equipment; food processing; lumber and wood products; machinery; metals; printed materials; scientific instruments; stone, clay, and glass products; transportation equipment.

Arkansas AR

25th State / June 15, 1836

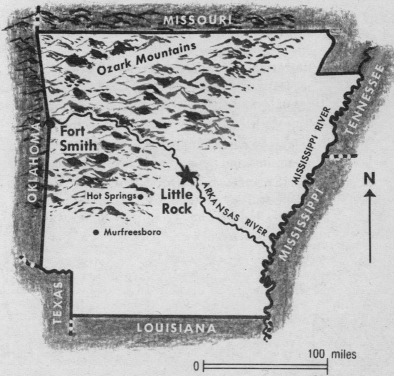

0 — 100 miles

0 — 160 kilometers

POPULATION 2,510,000
AREA 53,182 square miles
    137,742 square kilometers
FLOWER Apple blossom
TREE Pine
BIRD Mockingbird

◆ Most of the minerals found anywhere in the U.S. can also be found in Arkansas. More than 60 minerals are found in Magnet Cove, a valley near St. Francis.

About half the land in Arkansas is covered with forests. Many people come to Arkansas each year to see the beautiful mountains and lakes. Others come to visit Hot Springs. Some of them think the spring waters make sick people well.

Bill Clinton, the 42nd President, was born in Arkansas.

Pioneers had to make many things for themselves that people today can buy. At the Ozark Folk Center near Mountain View some people today are making things in the old ways. You can watch them work at the old crafts, hear them play the old mountain music. You can see old cabins built out of logs and wood shingles. Nearby is Blanchard Springs Caverns, one of the largest caves in the world.

Other things to see:

Arkansas Territorial Restoration — 14 buildings from before Arkansas was a state, in Little Rock

Crater of Diamonds State Park — where you can hunt for diamonds, "finders keepers," near Murfreesboro

Hot Springs National Park — more than a million gallons of hot mineral water every day from 47 springs

Museum of Automobiles — collection of antique cars, near Morrilton

Main Products

Agriculture: beef cattle, chickens, cotton, eggs, rice, soybeans, wood. Arkansas is first in broilers and a leader in forest products, rice, and soybeans.

Mining: bromine, natural gas, petroleum, stone. The state ranks first in the production of bromine and quartz.

Manufacturing: chemicals, clothing, electric and electronic equipment, food processing, furniture and fixtures, lumber and wood products, machinery, metals and metal products, paper products, plastic products, and shoes.

California CA

31st State / September 9, 1850

OREGON

LAKE TAHOE

SACRAMENTO RIVER

★ Sacramento

Oakland

San Francisco

SAN JOAQUIN RIVER

NEVADA

DEATH VALLEY

DESERT

MOJAVE DESERT

PACIFIC OCEAN

N

Los Angeles

COLORADO RIVER

ARIZONA

San Diego

100 miles

0

160 kilometers

MEXICO

POPULATION 31,878,000
AREA 163,707 square miles
        424,002 square kilometers
FLOWER Golden poppy
TREE California redwood
BIRD California valley quail

◆ Only two states — Alaska and Texas — are bigger than California.

Gold was found in California in 1848. People came by land and sea to dig for the gold. Today California has the most people in the U.S. More kinds of minerals are mined there than in any other state. California can grow more than 200 different crops. Almost all the almonds, dates, figs, olives, and raisins grown for market in the U.S. come from California.

The United Nations was founded in San Francisco in 1945. Many people in California work at finding new ways to do things. Many movies and TV shows come from the state.

Richard M. Nixon, 37th President, was born in California. Ronald Reagan, 40th President, was the state's governor.

Millions of people come to California each year. They visit the cities and ghost towns. They ski and swim. They walk among the redwoods — the tallest trees in the world — and the sequoia trees — the largest living things in the world.

Other things to see:

Death Valley — lowest place in U.S.

Disneyland — near Anaheim

La Brea Pits — bones of Ice Age animals stuck in oil and tar, at Los Angeles

Marine World Africa USA — oceanarium and wildlife park; shows by animals of sea, land and air, at Vallejo

Oroville Dam — highest earth-filled dam in U.S.

San Diego Harbor — home of U.S. Navy's Pacific Fleet

San Diego Zoo — one of the world's largest zoos

Yosemite National Park — canyons and waterfalls

Main Products

Agriculture: cattle, cotton, field crops, fruits and nuts, milk, nursery plants, poultry, vegetables. California is first in agriculture as a whole. Many crops are irrigated. The state is first in milk, grapes, peaches, plums, and many other fruits and vegetables.

Fishing: herring, rockfish, salmon, sea urchin, swordfish, tuna.

Mining: boron, cement, clays, gypsum, gold, limestone, petroleum, sand and gravel. California is third in petroleum. It has almost all the boron and the largest tungsten deposits in the U.S.

Manufacturing: aerospace communications and guidance systems, aircraft and spacecraft parts, computers and computer software, electronic components and accessories, food processing. California is first in manufacturing as a whole.

Colorado CO

38th State / August 1, 1876

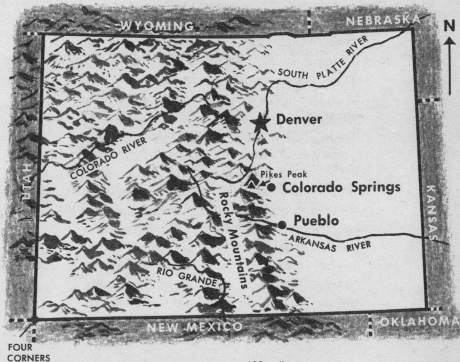

FOUR
CORNERS

0 — 100 miles
— 160 kilometers

POPULATION 3,823,000
AREA 104,100 square miles
269,620 square kilometers
FLOWER Rocky Mountain columbine
TREE Blue spruce
BIRD Lark bunting

◆More than 1,000 mountains in Colorado are over 10,000 feet (3,000 meters) high. There are plains in eastern Colorado. But even the plains are more than half a mile above sea level. The mountains of Colorado are known as a good place to ski.

Most of Colorado's people and farms are in the eastern part of the state. But most of the rain and snow fall on the west side of the mountains. Water is brought through the mountains in tunnels. It is used for homes, factories, and farms.

The city of Boulder owns Arapahoe Glacier. The glacier melts and the city uses the water. Boulder may be the only city in the world that owns a glacier.

Pikes Peak may be the most famous Rocky mountain. In 1893 Katherine Lee Bates went up Pikes Peak in a horse-drawn wagon. She took a good look from the top. Then she wrote the song "America the Beautiful." Today you can get to the top by car or cog railway.

Other things to see:

Air Force Academy — where officers are trained, near Colorado Springs

Bent's Old Fort National Historic Site — 1833 trading post

Black Canyon of the Gunnison National Monument — you can drive to the bottom of this deep, narrow gorge

Dinosaur beds — at Colorado and Dinosaur national monuments

Garden of the Gods — strange red rocks, at Colorado Springs

Ghost towns — from the gold and silver rush days, in the mountains

Mesa Verde National Park — Indian homes showing four different ways people lived from 1 A.D. to 1300 A.D.

Mount Evans Highway — highest paved road in the U.S.

Main Products

Agriculture: beef cattle, chickens, corn, flowers, hay, hogs, lamb, milk, sheep, vegetables, wheat, wool. Colorado is a leader in sheep. A lot of Colorado land is owned by the U.S. government. Some people graze their sheep and cattle on government land. They use some government land for logging and mining, too.

Mining: Coal, diamonds, gold, lead, molybdenum, natural gas, petroleum, sand and gravel, silver, stone, uranium, zinc. Colorado is second in molybdenum.

Manufacturing: chemicals; clothing; electronic equipment; food processing; machinery; printing and publishing; rubber and plastic products; scientific instruments; stone, clay, and glass products; transportation equipment; wood products.

Connecticut CT

5th State / January 9, 1788

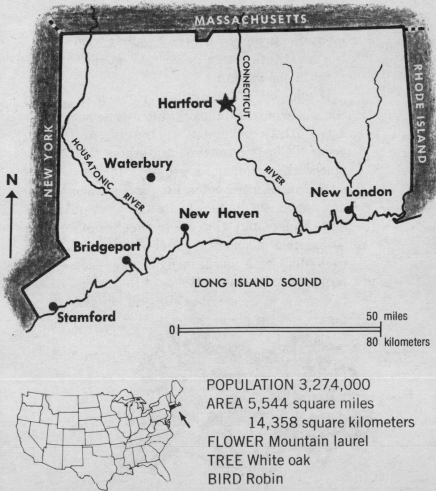

POPULATION 3,274,000
AREA 5,544 square miles
        14,358 square kilometers
FLOWER Mountain laurel
TREE White oak
BIRD Robin

◆ More than 100 years before our War of Independence, the Connecticut Colony passed a law giving voters the right to choose the people who ran the government. Some people call this the first written constitution of a democratic government in the world.

During our Constitutional Convention the men from the different states could not agree. The small states wanted as many votes in Congress as the large states. The states that had more people said they should have more votes. Roger Sherman of Connecticut came up with the answer. One house of Congress — the Senate — has two members from each state. So each small state gets as many votes as each large state. But in the House of Representatives a state's votes depend on the number of people in the state.

CHARTER
OAK

Much of Connecticut's land is not very good for farming. Many people live in pretty towns with old houses and churches and village greens.

Ever since colonial times Connecticut men have traveled far and wide selling things made in Connecticut. Eli Whitney made guns there. He made them so any part of one gun would fit any other gun he made. This was the beginning of mass production. Mass production made it possible for factories to make more goods for less money. Connecticut still has many factories.

Other things to see:

Mystic Seaport — whaling village and 100-year-old ships, at Mystic

Shore Line Trolley Museum — 100 classic trolleys; trolley rides, at East Haven

U.S.S. Nautilus — world's first nuclear-powered submarine, at Groton

Whitfield House — 1639 stone house in Guilford

35

Main Products

Agriculture: apples; eggs; milk; mushrooms; shrubs, flowers, vegetable plants; tobacco; wood. Connecticut's farmers grow a special tobacco that is used as the outside leaf on cigars.

Fishing: clams, flounder, lobster, oysters. Clams and oysters are grown in Long Island Sound.

Mining: clay, sand and gravel, stone.

Manufacturing: chemicals, electric and electronic equipment, instruments, machinery, metals and metal products, paper products, printed materials, rubber and plastic products, transportation equipment. Connecticut is a leader in submarines, jet aircraft engines, helicopters, ball bearings, and roller bearings.

Delaware DE

1st State / December 7, 1787

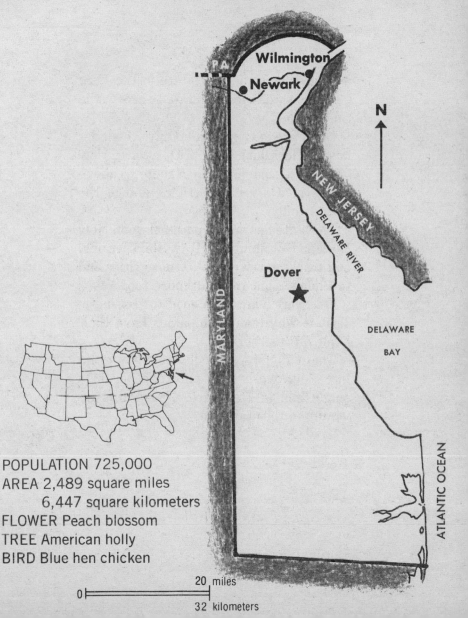

POPULATION 725,000
AREA 2,489 square miles
    6,447 square kilometers
FLOWER Peach blossom
TREE American holly
BIRD Blue hen chicken

Wilmington
Newark

N

PA

NEW JERSEY

DELAWARE RIVER

MARYLAND

Dover

DELAWARE BAY

ATLANTIC OCEAN

20 miles
0
32 kilometers

◆ Delaware is the first state in the U.S. because it was the first state to accept the Constitution.

Delaware is very small. Only Rhode Island has less land. Most of Delaware is low — no more than 60 feet (18 meters) above sea level. Only the northern end of the state is hilly.

The state lies on the path between New York and Washington, D.C. Ships, trains, and trucks carry goods to those cities and to Philadelphia and Baltimore too.

Delaware's laws are good for business. That is why many companies have their home offices there.

The many steps needed to make grain into flour were first put together in a single mill in Delaware. Nylon was invented in the state too.

Many colonial homes in Delaware are still lived in. Some towns set aside days when these homes may be visited.

Other things to see:

Hagley Museum — mills and small models show how water power was used by early American industry, at Wilmington

New Castle — old village green, colonial buildings, cobblestone streets

Odessa — 200-year-old houses

Old Swedes Church — oldest church (1698) in U.S. still in use, at Wilmington

Swedish log house — log cabin built in America (1638), Fort Christina State Park in Wilmington

Winterthur Museum — Almost 200 rooms of early American furniture, china, silver, from 1640 to 1840, near Wilmington

Main Products

Agriculture: chickens, corn, eggs, fruit, hogs, soybeans, vegetables. Delaware is a leader in broiler chickens.

Fishing: clams, crabs.

Mining: magnesium compounds, sand and gravel.

Manufacturing: chemicals, electric and electronic equipment, food processing, instruments, paper products, rubber and plastic products, printed materials. Delaware is called the "Chemical Capital of the World." Several important chemical companies have science research centers there. Some have factories in the state, too. Cars are built in Delaware. Many banks run their credit card divisions in Delaware.

Florida FL

27th State / March 3, 1845

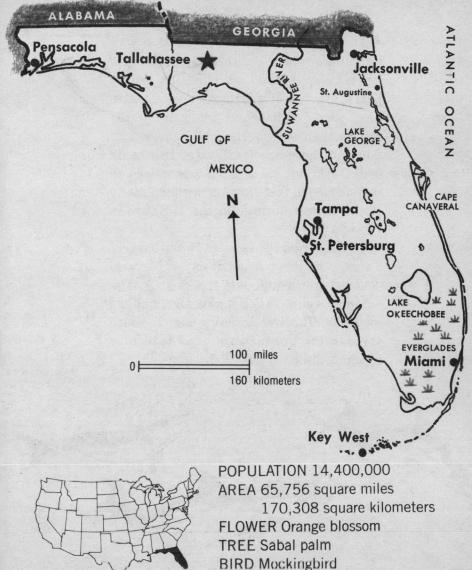

ALABAMA

GEORGIA

ATLANTIC OCEAN

Pensacola

Tallahassee ★

Jacksonville

St. Augustine

SUWANNEE RIVER

GULF OF

MEXICO

LAKE GEORGE

N

CAPE CANAVERAL

Tampa

St. Petersburg

LAKE OKEECHOBEE

EVERGLADES

Miami

100 miles

0

160 kilometers

Key West

POPULATION 14,400,000
AREA 65,756 square miles
     170,308 square kilometers
FLOWER Orange blossom
TREE Sabal palm
BIRD Mockingbird

41

◆The ocean goes almost all the way around Florida. The state has the second longest coast in the U.S. Most of Florida's land is low — just a little above the ocean. More kinds of fish are found in Florida waters than anywhere else in the world. Some of these are freshwater fish in its 30,000 lakes. Lots more water comes to the surface in fast-flowing springs. Many of the largest springs in the U.S. are in Florida.

The Everglades is one of the largest swamps in the world. It is part grass-covered prairie and part tree islands. The summer rains make Lake Okeechobee overflow. The water moves slowly south through the grass to the sea. In winter much of the Everglades dries up.

About 40 million people visit Florida each year. They fish, swim, water-ski, sail, and just lie in the sun. The Ringling Bros. and Barnum & Bailey Circus practices in Florida during the winter. Many baseball teams hold spring training there.

Other things to see:

Everglades National Park — bears, panthers, bobcats, alligators, crocodiles; Indian villages nearby

Horse farms — near Ocala

John F. Kennedy Space Center — at Cape Canaveral

John Pennekamp Coral Reef State Park — undersea park, 50 kinds of living coral, and wrecked ships on reefs

Key Deer National Wildlife Refuge — tiny deer the size of large dogs

Ringling Circus Gallery — at Sarasota

St. Augustine — oldest lasting European settlement in U.S., lived in since 1565

Sanibel Island — some of the best seashells in the world

Thomas A. Edison Home and Museum — inventor's winter home, at Ft. Myers

Walt Disney World/Epcot/MGM Disney — near Orlando

Main Products

Agriculture: beef cattle, fruit and nuts, honey, milk, plants, sugarcane, vegetables. Florida is first in oranges, grapefruit, tangerines, and nursery and greenhouse products. It is second in vegetables grown for market.

Fishing: blue crabs, catfish, clams, dolphin fish, grouper, mullet, oysters, pompano, red snapper, shrimp, spiny lobster, Spanish mackerel, stonecrabs, swordfish, tuna.

Mining: clays, limestone, natural gas, peat, petroleum, phosphate, sand, titanium. Florida is first in phosphate and titanium.

Manufacturing: chemicals, clothing, electric and electronic equipment, food processing, printed materials, transportation equipment, wood products.

Visitors are Florida's most important business.

Georgia GA

4th State / January 2, 1788

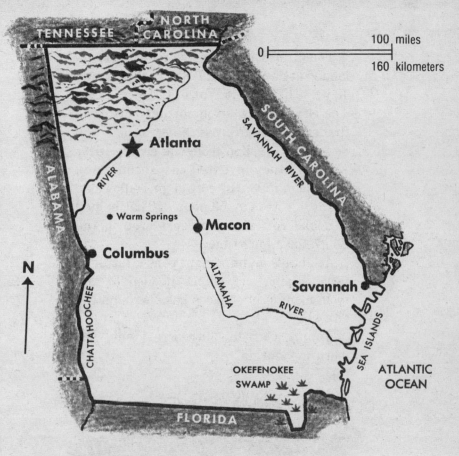

TENNESSEE

NORTH CAROLINA

SOUTH CAROLINA

0 |——————————| 100 miles
|——————————| 160 kilometers

ALABAMA

★ Atlanta

RIVER

SAVANNAH RIVER

● Warm Springs

● Macon

● Columbus

N ↑

CHATTAHOOCHEE

ALTAMAHA

Savannah

RIVER

SEA ISLANDS

OKEFENOKEE SWAMP

ATLANTIC OCEAN

FLORIDA

POPULATION 7,353,000
AREA 59,441 square miles
    153,953 square kilometers
FLOWER Cherokee rose
TREE Live oak
BIRD Brown thrasher

◆The first English settlers in Georgia landed at Savannah in 1733. That was only 42 years before our War of Independence. The city became an important port. The first steamship to cross the Atlantic — the *Savannah* — sailed from the city in 1819.

Eli Whitney invented the cotton gin in Georgia in 1793. His cotton gin could clean as much cotton as 50 people. That helped to make cotton the biggest crop in the South for a long time.

Atlanta is an important center for business. Trains and planes headed to and from many other places pass through the city.

Jimmy Carter, 39th President, was born in Georgia.

Georgia is the largest state east of the Mississippi River. Its Sea Islands are for everyone to enjoy. Once Jekyll Island was a private club for millionaires. Some of their homes can be visited now.

Other things to see:

Amicalola Falls — 729-foot (219-meter) waterfall, near Dawsonville

Gold Rush Museum — and several places to pan for gold, at Dahlonega

Ezekiel Harris House — 1797 tobacco merchant's house, at Augusta

Juliette Gordon Low Home — birthplace of founder of Girl Scouts of America, at Savannah

Little White House — a home of Franklin D. Roosevelt, our 32nd President, at Warm Springs

Ocmulgee National Monument — six different ways Indians lived from 8000 B.C. to 1717 A.D.; ruins and museum, near Macon

Okefenokee Swamp — largest freshwater swamp in U.S., alligators and other wildlife

Main Products

Agriculture: cattle, chickens, eggs, hogs, milk, peanuts, soybeans. Georgia is first in peanuts and pecans, and it is a leader in broiler chickens, eggs, cotton, peaches, and sweet potatoes. Forests cover almost two thirds of the state.

Fishing: blue crabs, shrimp.

Mining: barite, clays, sand and gravel, stone. Georgia is first in granite, kaolin, and marble.

Manufacturing: chemicals; clothing; electronic equipment; food processing; lumber and wood products; machinery; metal products; paper and paper products; printed materials; rubber and plastic products; stone, clay, and glass products; textiles; transportation equipment.

Hawaii HI

50th State / August 21, 1959

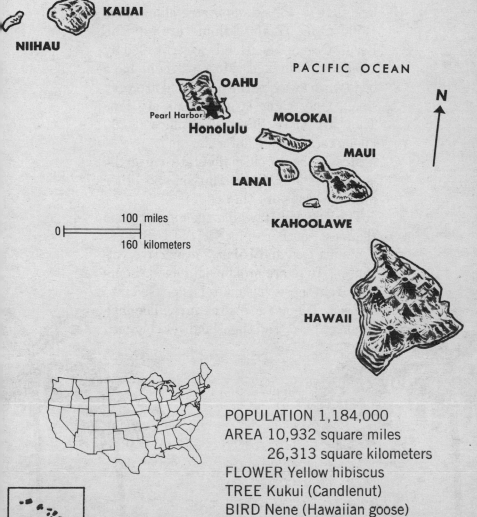

KAUAI

NIIHAU

PACIFIC OCEAN

OAHU

Pearl Harbor

Honolulu

MOLOKAI

N

MAUI

LANAI

KAHOOLAWE

100 miles

0

160 kilometers

HAWAII

POPULATION 1,184,000
AREA 10,932 square miles
      26,313 square kilometers
FLOWER Yellow hibiscus
TREE Kukui (Candlenut)
BIRD Nene (Hawaiian goose)

49

◆Hawaii is the only state made up of islands. It is 132 islands, stretching over 1,500 miles (2,400 kilometers) in the Pacific Ocean. The islands were formed by volcanoes long ago. Most of them have been worn away by the ocean and are very small. Only eight large islands are left. They are more than 2,000 miles (3,200 kilometers) from California.

Most of the people in the state live on the island of Oahu. Pearl Harbor and other military bases are there.

The island of Hawaii is the biggest. It is the most southern place in the U.S.

Mauna Loa and Kilauea are active volcanoes. They are on Hawaii Island. Some lava from these volcanoes has poured into the sea. The sea cools the lava. The lava becomes hard, and the island gets bigger.

The first people in Hawaii were Polynesians. They came in big canoes from other Pacific islands. Later Europeans, Asians, and Americans moved in. Its many different kinds of people help make Hawaii a very interesting place. Its weather makes the state a favorite vacation spot.

Other things to see:

Akaka Falls — 442 feet (133 meters), on Hawaii

Hawaii Volcanoes National Park — Mauna Loa, Kilauea crater, and a forest of giant ferns, on Hawaii

Mt. Waialeale — wettest place in the world with 460-inch (1,150-centimeter) average annual rainfall, on Kauai

Pearl Harbor — U.S. naval base; battleship *Arizona*, sunk December 7, 1941, on Oahu

Polynesian Cultural Center — people from six Pacific islands — Fiji, Tonga, Hawaii, New Zealand, Samoa, and Tahiti — live in villages, on Oahu

Waimea Canyon — the "Grand Canyon of Hawaii," on Kauai

Main Products

Agriculture: flowers and nursery products, macadamia nuts, melons, milk, pineapples, vegetables. Hawaii is the only state that grows coffee.

Fishing: tuna. Shrimp are raised in Hawaii.

Mining: pumice, sand and gravel, stone.

Manufacturing: clothing, food processing, stone, clay, and glass products.

The armed forces — army, navy, and air force — and visitors are both big businesses in Hawaii.

CANADA

N

Idaho ID

43rd State / July 3, 1890

0 |———————| 100 miles
160 kilometers

WASHINGTON

Rocky Mountains

MONTANA

SNAKE RIVER

SALMON RIVER

OREGON

Boise ★

SNAKE RIVER

WYOMING

Pocatello ●

NEVADA   UTAH

POPULATION 1,189,000
AREA 83,574 square miles
       216,456 square kilometers
FLOWER Syringa
TREE Western white pine
BIRD Mountain bluebird   53

◆Much of Idaho's fine farmland once looked like desert. The earth was very dry, but it was very rich. Idaho had many rivers, but the river water did not reach the dry land. Early farmers irrigated their fields. The water helped the "desert" grow crops. Today almost two out of three Idaho farms are irrigated.

Water makes most of the state's electricity too. Idaho has many dams on its rivers. They make electric power for homes and factories.

The first electricity from atomic energy was made in 1951 at the Idaho National Engineering Laboratory.

Idaho is full of beautiful mountains, lakes, rivers, and streams. People go there just to look and to take pictures. Some hunt deer, elk, and game birds. They catch enormous trout, huge sturgeon, and salmon. Other people look for precious and semi-precious stones all over the state. They float down the river rapids in rubber rafts. They visit hundreds of caves and many ghost towns. And they ski.

Other things to see:

Craters of the Moon National Monument — lava of many colors in strange shapes

Hells Canyon — cut by the Snake River to 7,900 feet (2,370 meters) — 1½ miles (2½ kilometers) — at its deepest point

Shoshone Falls — 212 feet (64 meters), near Twin Falls

Main Products

Agriculture: barley, beans, beef cattle, fruit, hay, hops, onions, potatoes, sheep, sugar beets, wheat. Idaho is first in potatoes and trout. More than half of Idaho's land is owned by the U.S. government.

Mining: garnets, gold, lead, molybdenum, phosphate, sand and gravel, silver. Idaho is first in antimony, garnets, and vanadium and a leader in lead.

Manufacturing: chemicals, electric and electronic equipment, food processing, lumber and wood products, machinery, paper products, printed materials. More than half of Idaho's potatoes are dried or frozen before they leave the state.

Illinois IL

21st State / December 3, 1818

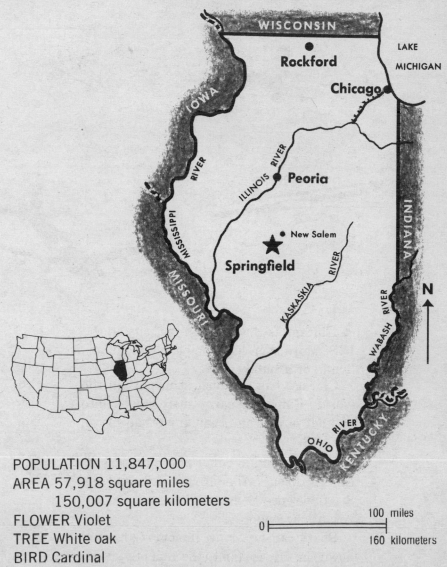

WISCONSIN

LAKE
MICHIGAN

IOWA

Rockford

Chicago

ILLINOIS RIVER

Peoria

MISSISSIPPI RIVER

New Salem

Springfield

KASKASKIA RIVER

INDIANA

WABASH RIVER

N

OHIO RIVER

KENTUCKY

MISSOURI

POPULATION 11,847,000
AREA 57,918 square miles
150,007 square kilometers
FLOWER Violet
TREE White oak
BIRD Cardinal

100 miles
0
160 kilometers

◆ Chicago is the third largest city in the U.S. More than half the people in Illinois live in or around the city.

Chicago has the busiest airport in the world. Railroads carry more goods into and out of Chicago than any other city in the U.S.

Chicago has a very busy port. Ships can go through the Great Lakes and the St. Lawrence Seaway all the way to the Atlantic Ocean.

Boats can go along Illinois rivers and down the Mississippi to the Gulf of Mexico.

Abraham Lincoln, 16th President, left Springfield, Illinois, to go to the White House. He was born in Kentucky and raised in Indiana. After he was grown up, he lived, worked, and studied in Illinois. For six years he lived in New Salem. You can see what that town was like when Lincoln was postmaster there.

Other things to see:

Chicago Museum of Science and Industry — see a coal mine, a submarine, and many other things

Field Museum of Natural History — animals in natural settings, at Chicago

Lincoln's home and tomb — at Springfield

Shedd Aquarium — all kinds of live fish, at Chicago

Ulysses S. Grant home — 18th President, at Galena

Zoos — Lincoln Park and Brookfield, both at Chicago

59

Main Products

Agriculture: beef cattle, corn, fruit, hay, hogs, milk, soybeans, vegetables. Illinois is often first in corn. Some years Iowa is first in corn. Then Illinois is second. It is a leader in hogs, cattle, and soybeans. Illinois is a very important farm state.

Mining: coal, fluorspar, petroleum, sand and gravel, stone. Illinois is first in fluorspar, and a leader in coal.

Manufacturing: chemicals, electric and electronic equipment, food processing, machinery, metals and metal products, printed materials, transportation equipment. Illinois is a leader in farm machinery, electrical products, iron and steel, candy, and many other products.

Indiana IN

19th State / December 11, 1816

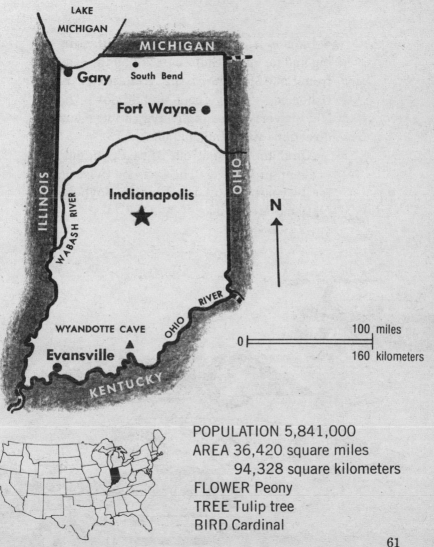

POPULATION 5,841,000
AREA 36,420 square miles
     94,328 square kilometers
FLOWER Peony
TREE Tulip tree
BIRD Cardinal

◆Indiana is a leader in both manufacturing and farming. Ships can sail all the way from Lake Michigan to the Atlantic Ocean. Other boats carry goods up and down the Ohio River. Super highways run in many directions from Indianapolis.

Abraham Lincoln, our 16th President, grew up in Indiana. The farm he lived on for 14 years is now the Lincoln Boyhood National Memorial.

Indiana has hills, lakes, forests, and flat farmland. It has sand dunes on the shore of Lake Michigan. Some of the dunes are now in the Indiana Dunes National Lakeshore.

Other things to see:

Benjamin Harrison National Historic Landmark — home of our 23rd President, at Indianapolis

Conner Prairie Pioneer Settlement — 1836 buildings and equipment; crafts, near Noblesville

Covered bridges — more than 30 in Parke County

Fort Ouiatenon — restored 1717 French fort, near Lafayette

Indianapolis Motor Speedway and Museum — where they run the 500-mile race; old winning cars

New Harmony — first place in U.S. where boys and girls were taught in the same classes

Santa Claus — a town that gets many important letters around Christmas time

Spring Mill State Park — 1816 village; grist mill, many shops and homes, near Mitchell

Wyandotte Caves — two separate caves, four different tours

Main Products

Agriculture: corn, hay, hogs, popcorn, soybeans, tobacco, wheat. Indiana is first in popcorn and a leader in corn, soybeans, tomatoes, chickens, ducks, and hogs.

Mining: clay, coal, gypsum stone, peat, petroleum, sand and gravel. The state is first in the production of building stone.

Manufacturing: chemicals, electrical equipment, food processing, machinery, metals and metal products, rubber and plastic products, transportation equipment. Indiana is first in steel. Great steel mills and oil refineries cover part of the Lake Michigan shore. Factories are found all through the state.

Iowa IA

29th State / December 28, 1846

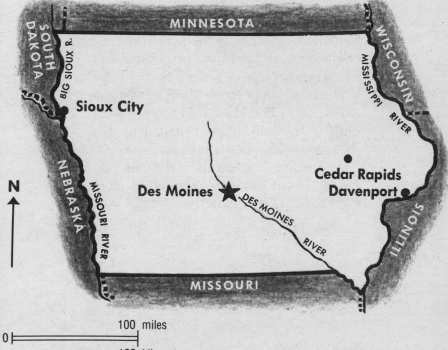

N

0 | 100 miles
160 kilometers

POPULATION 2,852,000
AREA 56,276 square miles
145,754 square kilometers
FLOWER Wild rose
TREE Oak
BIRD Eastern goldfinch

◆ Iowa has some of the best farmland in the U.S. Almost all of the land is used for farming. California is the only state that produces more food than Iowa. And California is nearly three times as big as Iowa!

The Mississippi River is on the east side of the state. The Missouri is on the west. Iowa is the only state bounded by two rivers that ships can travel on.

George Washington Carver studied science in Iowa. Later he thought up many ways to help farmers in the South.

People from many different countries came to Iowa to farm. Every year Iowa festivals are held to remember the old ways of living in those countries. And in August the only Indian tribe left in Iowa — the Mesquakie — has its pow-wow. The Iowa State Fair, one of the largest in the U.S., and the Annual Hobo Convention are held in August too.

Other things to see:

Fort Atkinson State Preserve — the only fort built to protect one Indian tribe from another

Herbert Hoover National Historic Site — birthplace of our 31st President, library, museum, at West Branch

Kalsow Prairie — the way all the prairie looked before it was plowed up, near Fort Dodge

Living History Farms — three working farms; one of the 1840's, one of the 1900's, and one of the future, near Des Moines

Wilder Museum — about 800 dolls; some are more than 200 years old, at Strawberry Point

Main Products

Agriculture: cattle, corn, hay, hogs, soybeans. Iowa is first in hogs and soybeans. It is often first in corn. Some years Illinois is first in corn. Then Iowa is second. Iowa is first in hogs and a leader in beef. Iowa feeds much of its corn to its hogs and cattle.

Mining: clay, gypsum, limestone, sand and gravel, shale.

Manufacturing: chemicals, electric and electronic equipment, food processing, machinery, metal products, printed materials, rubber and plastic products. Iowa has the biggest popcorn-packing plant in the U.S.

Insurance and helping people and companies manage their money are important businesses in Iowa.

Kansas KS

34th State / January 29, 1861

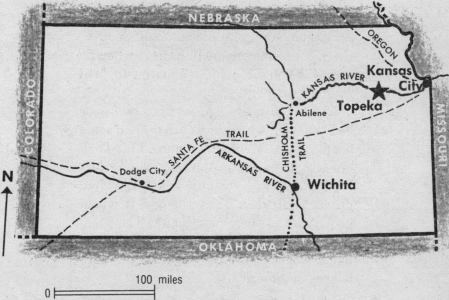

POPULATION 2,572,000
AREA 82,282 square miles
      213,110 square kilometers
FLOWER Sunflower
TREE Cottonwood
BIRD Western meadowlark

◆ Once there were millions and millions of buffalo on the plains. Some people shot them for fun from train windows. Others shot them for their hides. "Buffalo Bill" Cody got his nickname in Kansas when he shot 4,280 buffalo in 18 months to feed railroad workers.

About 100 years ago farmers had poor luck growing wheat in Kansas. Then some people called Mennonites moved in. They brought along a kind of wheat called "Turkey red." It was a winter wheat they had grown in Russia. They thought it would grow well in their new home. The Mennonites were right. Now Kansas grows so much wheat that it is called the "Breadbasket of America."

Abilene! Wichita! Dodge City! These cow towns are seen in movies and on TV. They had lawmen named Bat Masterson, Wyatt Earp, and "Wild Bill" Hickok. And exciting things really did happen in those towns a hundred years ago.

Today in Kansas the old and the new live side by side. Some of the old buildings can be visited in Dodge City and Wichita. And in Dodge City, cowboys on ATVs herd cattle in the stockyards.

Other things to see:

Eisenhower Library and Museum — and the boyhood home of our 34th President, in Abilene

Fort Larned National Historical Site — the fort was built to protect travelers on the Sante Fe Trail

Hollenberg Pony Express Museum — just as it looked in 1861, when horseback riders carried the mail, in Hanover

NCAA Visitors Center — displays of the 21 sports and 77 championships of the National Collegiate Athletic Association, in Overland Park

Main Products

Agriculture: beef cattle, corn, hogs, sorghum, soybeans, wheat. Kansas is the first state in sorghum and wheat and a leader in beef cattle.

Mining: helium, hydrogen, petroleum, natural gas, salt, sand and gravel, stone.

Manufacturing: chemicals, electric and electronic equipment, food processing, machinery, metal products, petroleum and coal products, printed materials, rubber and plastic products, transportation equipment. More than half the civilian airplanes in the U.S. are built in Wichita.

Kentucky KY

15th State / June 1, 1792

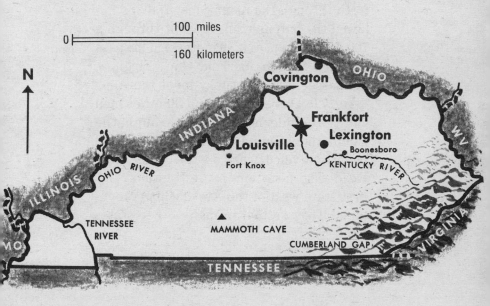

100 miles
0
160 kilometers

N

Covington
OHIO
INDIANA
WV
Frankfort
Lexington
Louisville
Boonesboro
Fort Knox
KENTUCKY RIVER
OHIO RIVER
ILLINOIS
VIRGINIA
MO
TENNESSEE RIVER
MAMMOTH CAVE
CUMBERLAND GAP
TENNESSEE

POPULATION 3,884,000
AREA 40,411 square miles
104,665 square kilometers
FLOWER Goldenrod
TREE Tulip poplar
BIRD Kentucky cardinal

73

◆Long ago buffalo wandered back and forth through the mountains. Indians followed the buffalo trail. It went through a 700-foot-deep pass (210 meters). This pass is called the Cumberland Gap. Virginia, Tennessee, and Kentucky meet there.

In 1775 Daniel Boone and 30 other men cut the Wilderness Road through the Cumberland Gap. Two hundred thousand people traveled west on the Wilderness Road. These settlers made Kentucky our first state west of the Appalachian Mountains. They settled in many other states too.

74

Kentucky has many mountains and lakes. There is fishing and small-game hunting. In Daniel Boone National Forest there is a special place to hunt with bows and arrows and muzzle-loading guns all year long.

Other things to see:

Abraham Lincoln Birthplace National Historic Site — where our 16th President was born

Cumberland Falls State Park — 68-foot (20-meter) waterfall that makes a "moonbow" — a kind of rainbow at night

Kentucky Horse Park — working horse farm and multi-media show on the history of the horse, Lexington

Mammoth Cave National Park — over 300 miles (480 kilometers) of passages, underground rivers, waterfalls, lakes

Old Fort Harrod — first lasting white settlement (1774), at Harrodsburg

Patton Museum of Cavalry and Armor — from War of Independence to present, at Fort Knox; you can see the outside of the building where most of the U.S. gold is kept.

75

Main Products

Agriculture: beef cattle, corn, eggs, hay, hogs, milk, soybeans, tobacco. Kentucky is second in tobacco. The state is famous for its thoroughbred horses and its bluegrass, a grass with blue flowers. Forests cover almost half the state.

Mining: coal, natural gas, petroleum, sand and gravel, stone. Kentucky is a leader in coal.

Manufacturing: chemicals, clothing, electric and electronic equipment, food processing, machinery, metals and metal products, paper products, printed materials, rubber and plastic products, tobacco products, transportation equipment. Kentucky is first in whiskey. The world's largest Braille publishing house is in Louisville.

Louisiana LA

18th State / April 30, 1812

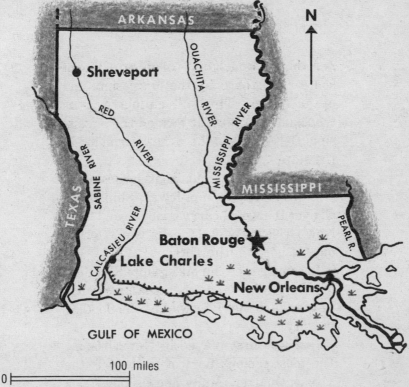

ARKANSAS

N

Shreveport

OUACHITA RIVER

RED RIVER

MISSISSIPPI RIVER

SABINE RIVER

TEXAS

MISSISSIPPI

CALCASIEU RIVER

PEARL R.

Baton Rouge

Lake Charles

New Orleans

GULF OF MEXICO

100 miles

0

160 kilometers

POPULATION 4,351,000
AREA 51,843 square miles
     134,275 square kilometers
FLOWER Magnolia
TREE Bald cypress
BIRD Brown pelican

77

◆ A third of Louisiana is made up of bits of soil carried there by the Mississippi and other rivers. The soil collected over thousands of years. It formed the Mississippi Delta. This is the richest farmland in the state.

New Orleans is Louisiana's largest city. It is on the Mississippi River. Ships from all over the world carry goods to and from New Orleans. New Orleans is one of the busiest ports in the U.S.

In some places the Mississippi River is 5 feet (1½ meters) higher than the city. Levees keep the river water from flooding the city.

Jazz was first played in New Orleans. The most famous part of the city is the French Quarter. Many houses there look like they did almost 200 years ago.

If you get to Louisiana, visit the Delta country. You can see fur trappers and fishermen living and working in the marshes. Many oil wells and sulfur mines are there too. And people say pirate treasure is hidden there.

Other things to see:

Grand Isle — where millions of birds rest every spring on their way home from their winter quarters

Jean Lafitte National Historical Park — where General Andrew Jackson's troops and the pirate band of Jean and Pierre Lafitte beat the British in the last battle of the War of 1812, near New Orleans

Lake Pontchartrain Causeway — longest bridge in the U.S. (24 miles or 38 kilometers), New Orleans

Levees and docks — New Orleans

Main Products

Agriculture: beef, cattle, chickens, cotton, eggs, rice, soybeans, sugarcane, wood. Louisiana is a leader in pecans, cotton, rice, sugarcane, and sweet potatoes. Forests cover about one-third of the state.

Fishing; catfish, crawfish, menhaden, oysters, shrimp.

Mining: lignite, natural gas, petroleum, salt, sulfur. Louisiana is first in salt and sulfur, second in natural gas, and a leader in petroleum. Clam shells are dredged from lakes and used in construction materials.

Furs: Louisiana is a leader in wild animal skins, such as nutria.

Manufacturing: chemicals, food processing, lumber and wood products, machinery, metal products, paper products, petroleum and coal products, printing and publishing, transportation equipment.

Maine ME

23rd State / March 15, 1820

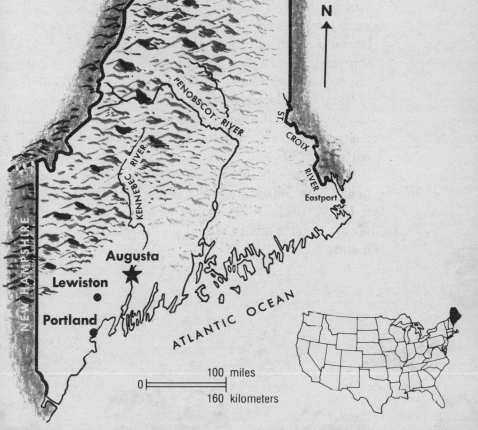

CANADA

N

PENOBSCOT RIVER

KENNEBEC RIVER

ST. CROIX RIVER

Eastport

NEW HAMPSHIRE

Augusta

Lewiston

Portland

ATLANTIC OCEAN

0   100 miles
     160 kilometers

POPULATION 1,243,000
AREA 35,387 square miles
      91,653 square kilometers

FLOWER White pine cone and tassel
TREE White pine
BIRD Chickadee

◆In 1607 an English colony was started at the mouth of the Kennebec River. Life was too hard. The people soon left. But while they lived there, they built the *Virginia*, the first successful ocean-going ship made in America. The *Virginia* sailed the seas for 20 years.

Maine people have always built ships. Large ships and small boats are built in many towns. Submarines are rebuilt in Kittery.

Maine once belonged to one English family. The Massachusetts Colony bought it for $6,000 in 1677. Maine was part of Massachusetts until 1819. Then it became a state too.

Maine is a famous vacationland. People come to Maine to hike, climb mountains, and ski. They sail among the 400 coastal islands. They paddle canoes on lakes and ponds, rivers and streams. They hunt deer and bear.

A large part of Maine has no roads. Some people travel in canoes and in planes that land on lakes.

Acadia National Park is the only national park where the mountains meet the sea. It is the first one made up of land given to the government. The park gets larger as new gifts are added.

Other things to see:

Burnham Tavern — where Americans plotted the first naval battle of the War of Independence, at Machias

Passamaquoddy Bay — highest tides off U.S. mainland

Portland Head Light — President George Washington had this lighthouse built, near Portland

Main Products

Agriculture: apples, beef cattle, blueberries, eggs, milk, potatoes, wood. Maine is a leader in potatoes. Forests cover almost all of the state. Each year about a million firs are cut down for Christmas trees.

Fishing: clams, cod, cusk, flounder, haddock, hake, halibut, lobster, ocean perch, scallops, sea urchins, shrimp, worms. Maine is first in lobster and sardines.

Mining: gemstones, sand and gravel, stone.

Manufacturing: electric and electronic equipment, food processing, leather products, lumber and wood products, machinery, pulp and paper, ships and boats, textiles. Maine is first in wooden toothpicks.

Maryland MD

7th State / April 28, 1788

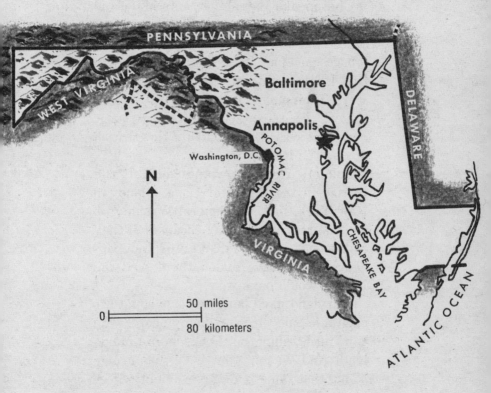

POPULATION 5,072,000
AREA 12,407 square miles
    32,135 square kilometers
FLOWER Black-eyed Susan
TREE White oak
BIRD Baltimore oriole

FABULOUS FACT "The Star-Spangled Banner"
was written while the British attacked
Baltimore's Fort McHenry during the War of 1812.

◆ Chesapeake Bay almost cuts Maryland in two. Many rivers run into the bay. Baltimore was started on one of the rivers as a tobacco port for northern Maryland farms. But it grew into a city when farmers started shipping wheat from its port. Baltimore was the only important Atlantic port that was never held by the British during the Revolution.

Soldiers from Maryland held off the British in the Battle of Long Island, in New York, in 1776. General Washington and the rest of the army escaped. If they had been caught, our War of Independence might have ended then. And the British would have won.

Maryland gave land that our country's capital is built on. Now many people who work in Washington, D.C., live in Maryland. And Washington, D.C., has grown so big that some U.S. government offices are in Maryland.

Maryland has many fine buildings that were built as much as 200 years ago. Maryland's state sport is old too. It is called jousting. Every year there are jousting tournaments. People on horseback try to catch rings on their lances.

Other things to see:

Fort McHenry National Monument — "The Star-Spangled Banner" was written about the battle for this fort in 1814.

B & O Railroad Museum — Mount Clare Station, first railroad station (1830) in U.S., at Baltimore

State House — built in 1779, oldest still in use in U.S.; Congress met here in 1783-84, at Annapolis

U.S. Frigate *Constellation* — oldest ship still afloat, at Baltimore

U.S. Naval Academy — where officers are trained, at Annapolis

87

Main Products

Agriculture: cattle, chickens, corn, fruit, greenhouse and nursery products, milk, soybeans.

Fishing: blue crabs, oysters, soft shell clams. Striped bass are raised on fish farms.

Mining: clays, coal, sand and gravel, stone.

Manufacturing: chemicals, electric and electronic equipment, food processing, machinery, printing and publishing, transportation equipment. Baltimore has long been a world port.

Many people in Maryland do research to find out more about computers and software, space flight, health, and new ways to farm.

Massachusetts MA

6th State / February 6, 1788

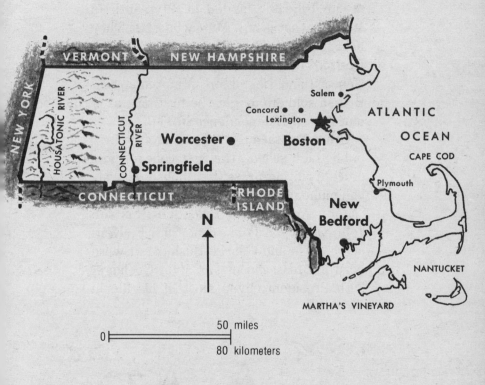

VERMONT   NEW HAMPSHIRE

NEW YORK

HOUSATONIC RIVER

CONNECTICUT RIVER

Salem

Concord ● ● Lexington

★ Boston

ATLANTIC OCEAN

CAPE COD

Worcester ●

● **Springfield**

CONNECTICUT

RHODE ISLAND

Plymouth ●

New Bedford ●

N

NANTUCKET

MARTHA'S VINEYARD

0   50 miles
        80 kilometers

POPULATION 6,092,000
AREA 10,555 square miles
       27,337 square kilometers
FLOWER Mayflower
TREE American elm
BIRD Chickadee

89

◆The Pilgrims landed at Plymouth in 1620, in what is now Massachusetts. They held their first Thanksgiving in 1621. The Boston Tea Party took place in 1773. At Concord and Lexington, Minutemen and British soldiers fought the first battles of our War of Independence in 1775.

Other Massachusetts firsts are the first public high school, the first college, post office, printing press, lighthouse, basketball game, and subway in America.

John Adams, 2nd President; his son John Quincy Adams, 6th; John F. Kennedy, 35th; and George Bush, 41st, were born in Massachusetts. Calvin Coolidge, 30th President, lived most of his life in the state.

For skiing, music, and dance, visit western Massachusetts; for history and seashore, the east coast.

Other things to see:

Boston — Bunker Hill, Paul Revere's House, Old North Church, Faneuil Hall, *Old Ironsides*, and places where the Boston Massacre and Boston Tea Party took place

Cape Cod National Seashore — beautiful sand dunes, nature walks

Old Sturbridge Village — see how people lived about 150 years ago; craft shows and farm animals

Plymouth — see how the Pilgrims lived at Plimoth Plantation and where people say they landed at Plymouth Rock.

Salem — Maritime National Historic Site and Witch House

Saugus Iron Works National Historic Site — where U.S. steel industry began

Whaling Museum — at New Bedford

Main Products

Agriculture: eggs, flowers and shrubs, fruit, milk, turkeys, vegetables. Massachusetts is usually first in cranberries. Forests cover more than half the state.

Fishing: bluefish, cod, flounder, haddock, herring, lobster, mackerel, menhaden, ocean pout, pollock, scallops, sea bass, squid, swordfish. Massachusetts is a leader in fishing and particularly in sea scallops. Trout and striped bass are grown on fish farms.

Mining: lime, sand and gravel, stone.

Manufacturing: chemicals, clothing, computer hardware and software, electric and electronic equipment, instruments, machinery, metal products, plastics, printed materials, textiles. Massachusetts is a leader in software and hardware for computers. The first American factories in many different industries were built in Massachusetts. Now there is a lot of medical and other kinds of research done in this state.

Education and helping people and companies manage their money are important businesses in Massachusetts.

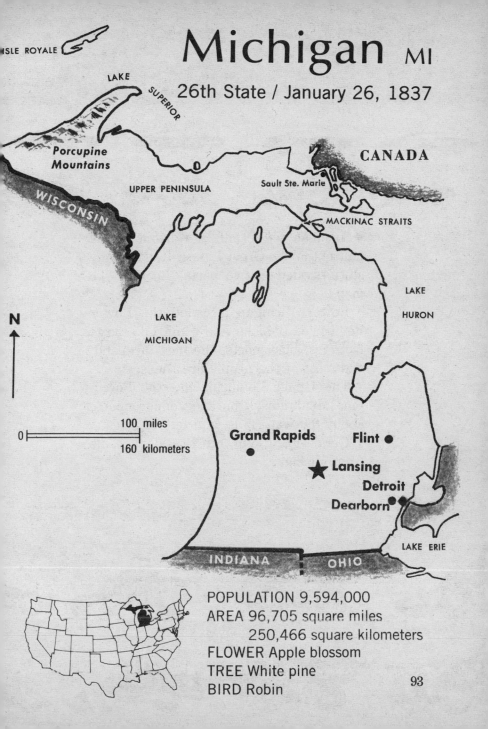

ISLE ROYALE

Michigan MI

26th State / January 26, 1837

LAKE SUPERIOR

CANADA

Porcupine Mountains

UPPER PENINSULA

Sault Ste. Marie

WISCONSIN

MACKINAC STRAITS

LAKE HURON

N

LAKE MICHIGAN

0   100 miles
    160 kilometers

Grand Rapids •

Flint •

★ Lansing

Detroit •
Dearborn •

LAKE ERIE

INDIANA   OHIO

POPULATION 9,594,000
AREA 96,705 square miles
     250,466 square kilometers
FLOWER Apple blossom
TREE White pine
BIRD Robin

93

◆Michigan is the only state touched by four of the five Great Lakes. It is the only state divided in two parts. Look at the map.

Lower Michigan is called the Lower Peninsula. It looks like a mitten. Large factories, busy ports, the best farmland, and most of the people are there.

The Upper Peninsula has the Porcupine Mountains, iron and copper mines, about 150 waterfalls, and lots of forests.

Gerald Ford, our 38th President, came from Michigan.

Michigan has 11,000 lakes and tens of thousands of campsites. People come to hunt, fish, ski, swim, and boat. One of the world's highest man-made ski flying slides is at Copper Peak, near Ironwood.

At Greenfield Village in Dearborn you can see what Thomas A. Edison's laboratory and the Wright brothers' bicycle shop looked like. Craft shops at Greenfield Village show how early Americans used hand tools.

Other things to see:

Isle Royale National Park — wilderness area with a moose herd and timber wolves, in Lake Superior

Mackinac Bridge — world's longest suspension bridge (5 miles or 8 kilometers) connects upper and lower Michigan

Soo Canals — giant locks let giant ships pass between Lake Superior and Lake Huron, at Sault Ste. Marie

Windmill Island Municipal Park — only real Dutch windmill in the U.S., grinds flour, at Holland

Main Products

Agriculture: apples, beef cattle, blueberries, cherries, cucumbers, dry beans, eggs, greenhouse and nursery products, hogs, horses, milk. Michigan is first in blueberries, red tart cherries, dry beans, Easter lilies, geraniums, and cucumbers for pickles. Almost half the state is covered by forests.

Fishing: catfish, chub, whitefish. Perch and trout are grown on fish farms.

Mining: bromine, gypsum, iron ore, natural gas, petroleum, sand and gravel, stone. Michigan is second in iron ore, peat, and sand and gravel. Many mining products are taken from natural brine.

Manufacturing: chemicals, electric and electronic equipment, food processing, furniture and fixtures, machinery, metals and metal products, rubber and plastic products, transportation equipment. Michigan is first in automobiles. Battle Creek makes more breakfast cereal than any other city in the world.

Visitors are important to Michigan.

Minnesota MN

32nd State / May 11, 1858

CANADA

LAKE BEMIDJI

Hibbing

MESABI RANGE

LAKE SUPERIOR

LAKE ITASCA

NORTH DAKOTA

RED RIVER OF THE NORTH

Duluth

MISSISSIPPI RIVER

0   100 miles

160 kilometer

Minneapolis

St. Paul

MINNESOTA RIVER

WISCONSIN

SOUTH DAKOTA

N

Rochester ●

IOWA

POPULATION 4,658,000
AREA 86,943 square miles
    225,182 square kilometers
FLOWER Pink and white lady's-slipper
TREE Norway pine
BIRD Common loon

97

◆Minneapolis and St. Paul are called Twin Cities. They are right across the Mississippi River from each other. Boats carry goods down the Mississippi from these busy cities. They can go all the way down to New Orleans.

Minnesota's iron ore travels on huge ships. They sail from Duluth, across Lake Superior. The ships pass through the locks at Sault Ste. Marie in Michigan. Then the ore can be taken to the giant steel mills of Illinois, Indiana, Ohio, and Pennsylvania.

One of the world's great medical centers is the Mayo Clinic in Rochester. Research is done there to find new ways to make people healthy.

98

Millions of people vacation in Minnesota each year. They swim, fish, and boat on more than 15,000 lakes. They hunt in the deep forests. In winter they ski and snowmobile, ice-fish and skate.

Other things to see:

Biggest man-made hole in the world — an open-pit iron mine, at Hibbing

Fort Snelling — 1820's fort, near St. Paul

Grand Portage National Monument — 1768 fur-trading post

Lake Itasca State Park — wade across the stream that grows to be the mighty Mississippi River

Lumbertown, U.S.A. — pioneer lumbering village, near Brainerd

Statues of folk hero Paul Bunyan — the giant lumberjack and his blue ox, Babe; at Bemidji, Brainerd, and Akeleg

Main Products

Agriculture: barley, beef cattle, chickens, corn, dry beans, eggs, hay, hogs, milk, oats, potatoes, soybeans, sugar beets, sunflowers, turkeys, vegetables, wheat, wood. Minnesota is first in sugar beets. It is a leader in milk, corn, hay, hogs, oats, soybeans, and turkeys.

Fishing: buffalo fish, carp, catfish, walleye, whitefish, and yellow perch.

Mining: iron ore, sand and gravel, stone. More than three quarters of U.S. iron ore is mined in Minnesota.

Manufacturing: chemicals, electric and electronic equipment; food processing; instruments; lumber and wood products; machinery; metal products; printed materials; pulp and paper products; rubber and plastic products; stone, clay, and glass products; transportation equipment. Minnesota is a leader in cheese, butter, dry milk, canned vegetables, and meat.

Mississippi MS

20th State / December 10, 1817

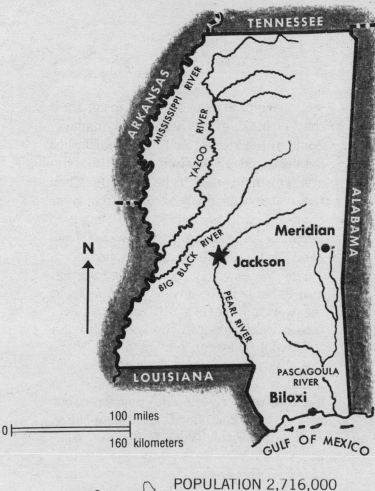

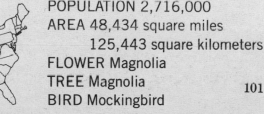

POPULATION 2,716,000
AREA 48,434 square miles
        125,443 square kilometers
FLOWER Magnolia
TREE Magnolia
BIRD Mockingbird

101

◆Mississippi is named for the great river that is most of its western boundary. Some of the richest soil in the world lies between the Mississippi and Yazoo rivers. This land used to be swampy. Then the water was drained off. High river banks called levees were built. They help keep the Mississippi River water from overflowing and flooding the land.

The Waterways Experiment Station near Jackson is the largest river model in the world. It covers 210 acres (84 hectares). Engineers can run water through the model. They can see when and where the Mississippi and its feeder rivers will overflow. Then they warn the people who live near those rivers. They also figure out new ways to keep floods from happening. Now a lot of this work is done on computers.

Flatboats carried goods down the Mississippi before there were railroads and trucks. But the boats could not go up the river. The boatmen used the Natchez Trace, a road that followed an old Indian trail. It took them back to the Ohio and Tennessee rivers. Today you can drive on the Natchez Trace Parkway. Near the road you can see a Choctaw Indian village, the second largest petrified forest in the U.S., and the Mississippi River Basin model.

Other things to see:

Florewood River Plantation — how people lived on a cotton plantation; weaving, soap and candle making, at Greenwood

John Ford House — early 1800's frontier home, with 1826 additions, near Sandy Hook

Old Spanish Fort and Singing River — at Pascagoula

Main Products

Agriculture: beef cattle, chickens, cotton, eggs, milk, rice, soybeans, vegetables, wood. Mississippi has more tree farms than any other state. It is a leader in cotton. More than half the land is covered by forests.

Fishing: menhaden, oysters, red snapper, shrimp. Mississippi is first in catfish raised for market.

Mining: clays, natural gas, petroleum, sand and gravel.

Manufacturing: chemicals, clothing, electrical equipment, food processing, furniture and fixtures, lumber and wood products, machinery, paper products, petroleum products, transportation equipment, wood products. The largest manufacturer of guitar amplifiers is in Meridian.

Missouri MO

24th State / August 10, 1821

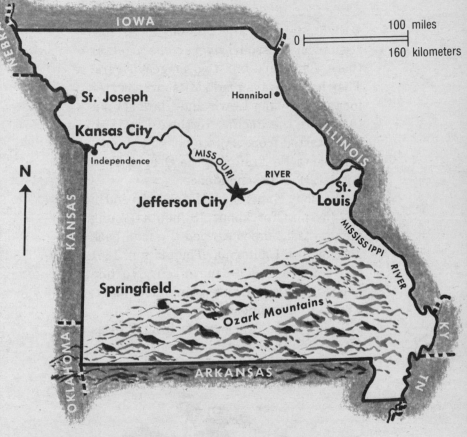

IOWA

NEBRASKA

100 miles
0 ⊢——————⊣
160 kilometers

St. Joseph

Hannibal •

Kansas City

ILLINOIS

Independence

MISSOURI   RIVER

N
↑

KANSAS

Jefferson City

St. Louis

MISSISSIPPI   RIVER

Springfield •

Ozark Mountains

KY

OKLAHOMA

ARKANSAS

TN

POPULATION 5,359,000
AREA 69,709 square miles
     180,546 square kilometers
FLOWER Hawthorn
TREE Flowering dogwood
BIRD Bluebird

105

◆Eight states border Missouri. The Mississippi and Missouri rivers come together there. They are our two longest rivers. They have always made Missouri a center for travel. When Lewis and Clark set out to explore the Pacific Northwest in 1804, they started from a place near St. Louis. The Santa Fe Trail and the Oregon Trail both start in Independence.

The Pony Express had its eastern end in St. Joseph. For about 18 months young men on fast horses carried the mail back and forth to California. Then late in 1861 the telegraph was invented. No one needed the Pony Express any more and it went out of business.

Today boats carry goods from Kansas City and St. Louis. And their airports are among the busiest in the U.S.

The Ozarks in southern Missouri are low mountains and hills covered by forests. The Ozarks' fast streams, large springs and lakes, and deep caves bring many visitors to the state. In July young people try to win the National Tom Sawyer Fence Painting Contest in Hannibal.

Other things to see:

Fort Osage — first U.S. fort in Louisiana Territory, near Sibley

Gateway Arch — tallest monument built in U.S. (630 feet or 192 meters); ride in small cars to the top, at the Jefferson National Expansion Memorial at St. Louis

George Washington Carver National Monument — birthplace of the great black scientist, near Diamond

Harry S. Truman Birthplace — where our 33rd President was born, at Lamar

Mark Twain's Boyhood Home and Museum — at Hannibal

Pony Express Stables and Museum — at St. Joseph

Ste. Genevieve — oldest (1735) lasting white settlement in Missouri

Main Products

Agriculture: beef cattle, corn, cotton, hay, hogs, milk, rice, sorghum, soybeans, wheat. Missouri is an important farm state. It is a leader in corn, sorghum, and soybeans. Much of its corn, small grains, and hay are fed to its cattle and hogs.

Mining: coal, iron ore, lead, stone, zinc. Missouri is first in lead and fire clay, second in iron oxide, and third in barite, iron, and stone.

Manufacturing: chemicals, electric and electronic equipment, food processing, machinery, metal products, printed materials, transportation equipment. Many of Missouri's factories are in St. Louis and Kansas City. The state is a leader in automobiles, beer, greeting cards, and meat-packing. One of the largest dairy-processing plants in the U.S. is in Springfield.

Montana MT

41st State / November 8, 1889

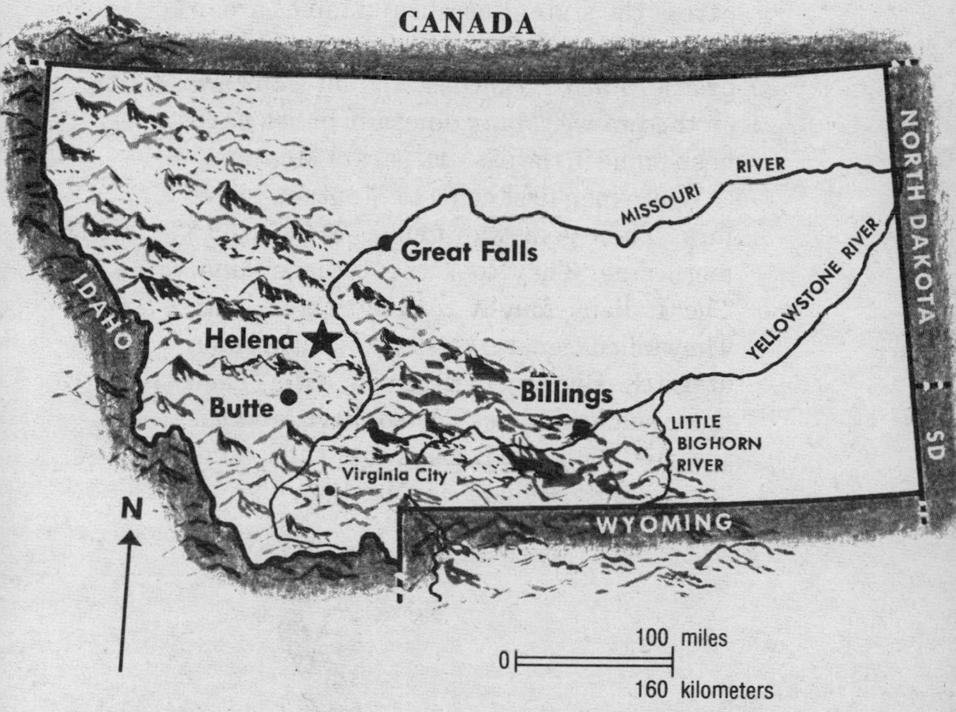

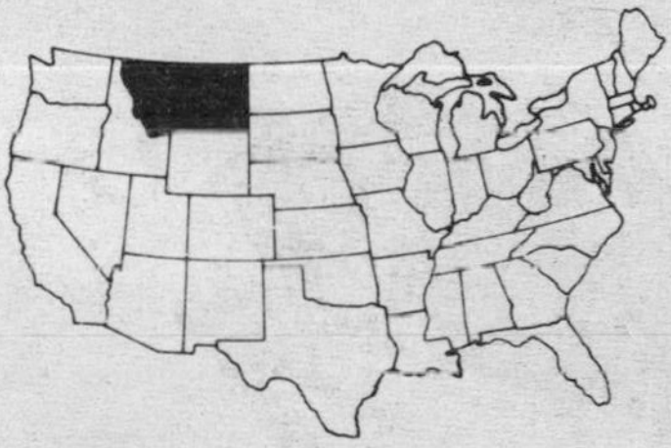

CANADA

IDAHO

NORTH DAKOTA

SD

MISSOURI RIVER

YELLOWSTONE RIVER

Great Falls

Helena ★

Butte

Billings

Virginia City

LITTLE BIG HORN RIVER

WYOMING

N

0 ____ 100 miles

160 kilometers

POPULATION 879,000
AREA 147,046 square miles
　　　　380,850 square kilometers
FLOWER Bitterroot
TREE Ponderosa pine
BIRD Western meadowlark

◆Montana is a Spanish word for mountain. The Rocky Mountains are in the western part of the state. Forests and mines are in the mountains. The rest of the land is prairie. Farms, ranches, and oil wells are on the prairie. Many dinosaur bones have been found in the eastern part of Montana.

White men first came to Montana to get furs. Then gold was found. More white men came. They took the Indians' land. The Indians fought to keep their land. They killed General Custer and all his men at Little Big Horn River in 1876. Then more soldiers came. The soldiers beat the Indians. And the Indians lost their land. Today most Indians in Montana live on reservations.

Many towns in Montana have rodeos. Indian crafts and ceremonies can be seen at seven reservations. Hunting, fishing, and skiing all have their fans. You can search for precious and semi-precious stones and visit many ghost towns.

Other things to see:

Big Horn Canyon — almost 3,000 feet (900 meters) deep

Berkeley Pit — huge open-pit copper mine, at Butte

Custer Battlefield National Monument

Glacier National Park —about 60 glaciers and 200 lakes; deer, elk, bears, mountain goats

Medicine Rocks — sandstone buttes made into strange shapes by wind and rain

National Bison Range — about 500 buffalo, at Dixon

Main Products

Agriculture: barley, beef cattle, hay, sheep, sugar beets, wheat, wood, wool. Many Christmas trees are cut in Montana each year.

Mining: coal, copper, gemstones, gold, natural gas, petroleum, platinum-palladium, silver, zinc. Montana is first in talc and the only state producing platinum. Gold, silver, and zinc are often found with Montana's copper. The state has a lot of coal. The U.S. government controls almost half the mineral rights in Montana.

Manufacturing: chemicals, food processing, lumber and wood products, metals, petroleum and coal products.

The most important business in Montana is agriculture. The second is visitors.

Nebraska NE

37th State / March 1, 1867

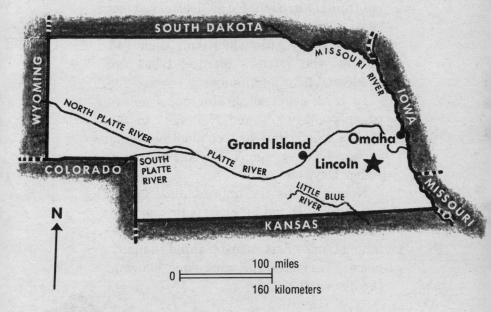

SOUTH DAKOTA

MISSOURI RIVER

WYOMING

IOWA

NORTH PLATTE RIVER

Grand Island

Omaha

COLORADO

SOUTH PLATTE RIVER

PLATTE RIVER

Lincoln ★

LITTLE BLUE RIVER

MISSOURI

N

KANSAS

0	100 miles
	160 kilometers

POPULATION 1,652,000
AREA 77,358 square miles
      200,358 square kilometers
FLOWER Goldenrod
TREE Cottonwood
BIRD Western meadowlark

◆Most early settlers in Nebraska had no wood to build their houses. There were not many trees in Nebraska then. So most people built huts made of sod. Sod is earth cut from the ground. Each block of sod has roots of grasses in it. The roots hold the sod together. After they built their sod houses, the settlers planted trees for shade and fruit and lumber.

In 1872, J. Sterling Morton, a newspaper publisher, asked Nebraska to set aside a special day for tree planting. Now people all over the U.S. plant trees on Arbor Day.

Nebraska has the only national forest completely planted by man. It proved that forests could grow on the Plains. Now large stands of trees are planted in many places. They stop the wind from blowing the dry earth away.

Nebraska was once called the Great American Desert. Pioneers passed straight through on their way to Oregon, Utah, and California. Then people began to graze cattle on the wild grasses. They planted wheat in the west and corn in the east. Now Nebraska is one of our leading farm states.

Other things to see:

Agate Fossil Beds National Monument — "stone bones" of many animals, near Scottsbluff

Fort Niobrara National Wildlife Refuge — buffalo and many other wild animals, Texas longhorns

Pioneer Village — sod hut and many other early buildings; crafts

Scout's Rest Ranch — Buffalo Bill Cody's home; Wild West Show training grounds, at North Platte

115

Main Products

Agriculture: beef cattle, corn, hay, hogs, sorghum, soybeans, sugar beets, wheat. Nebraska is first in great northern beans and a leader in corn and beef cattle. Agriculture is the state's most important business.

Mining: natural gas, petroleum, sand and gravel.

Manufacturing: chemicals, electric and electronic equipment, food processing, instruments, machinery, metals and metal products, transportation equipment. Nebraska is one of the country's largest meat-packing centers. Many insurance companies have their headquarters in Nebraska.

Nevada NV

36th State / October 31, 1864

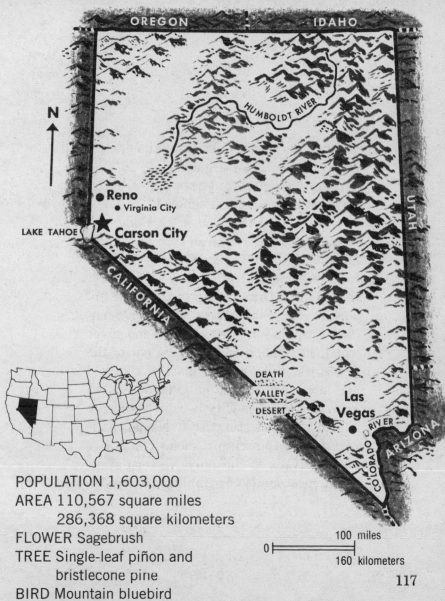

OREGON　　　IDAHO

N

HUMBOLDT RIVER

● Reno
● Virginia City

LAKE TAHOE

★ **Carson City**

CALIFORNIA

UTAH

DEATH
VALLEY
DESERT

**Las
Vegas**

COLORADO RIVER

ARIZONA

POPULATION 1,603,000
AREA 110,567 square miles
　　　286,368 square kilometers
FLOWER Sagebrush
TREE Single-leaf piñon and
　　　bristlecone pine
BIRD Mountain bluebird

100 miles

0 ⊢———————

160 kilometers

117

◆ Nevada is mostly mountains and desert. It did not look like a good place to live. Settlers passed through as fast as they could on their way to California.

Then in 1859 the Comstock Lode was discovered. The lode was gold and silver mixed together. Thousands rushed there to strike it rich. Virginia City was settled. Overnight it became one of the most important cities in the West. Only San Francisco was more important. Gold and silver worth 300 million dollars came out of the Comstock. But by 1880 most of the gold and silver ore was gone. People drifted away and Virginia City became a village.

Today millions still rush to Nevada each year to try to strike it rich. That's because Nevada is the only western state where most kinds of gambling are legal.

Many people come to Nevada to gamble and to see the stars who give shows there. Most Nevadans live around Las Vegas and Reno. That leaves plenty of country for people to hunt and fish in. They ski on the high mountains. They water-ski and swim. They visit old mining camps, like Virginia City, and many other ghost towns.

Other things to see:

Bristlecone Pines — oldest living things in the world, some more than 4,000 years old, in Great Basin National Park

Geyser Basin — hot springs and mud pools, near Beowawe

Hoover Dam — the second highest dam in the U.S.

Lehman Caves National Monument — limestone caverns, near Baker

119

Main Products

Agriculture: beef cattle, greenery and nursery products, hay, milk, potatoes. Nevada gets little rain. Farmers need to irrigate. Cattle graze on government land. Most of Nevada is owned by the U.S. government.

Mining: barite, copper, diatomite, gold, gypsum, lime, lithium, mercury, petroleum, silver. Nevada is first in both gold and silver.

Manufacturing: electric and electronic equipment; food processing; instruments; machinery; metal products; printed materials; rubber and plastic products; stone, clay, and glass products.

The most important business in Nevada is visitors.

New Hampshire NH

9th State / June 21, 1788

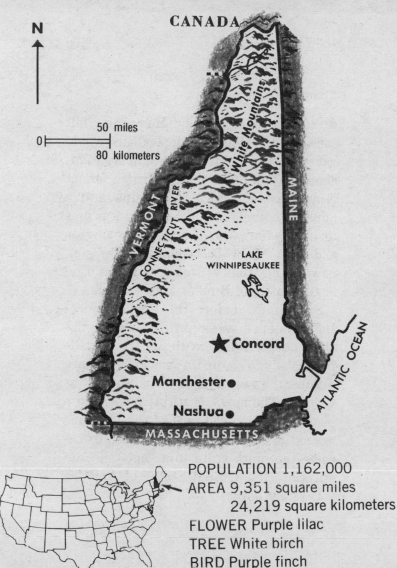

CANADA

N

50 miles
0
80 kilometers

VERMONT

CONNECTICUT RIVER

White Mountains

MAINE

LAKE
WINNIPESAUKEE

★ Concord

Manchester ●

Nashua ●

ATLANTIC OCEAN

MASSACHUSETTS

POPULATION 1,162,000
AREA 9,351 square miles
        24,219 square kilometers
FLOWER Purple lilac
TREE White birch
BIRD Purple finch

◆ Some people in New Hampshire felt sure that the War of Independence would have to be fought. In December, 1774, about 400 men attacked a British fort at New Castle. They took guns and a hundred barrels of powder. This was four months before the battles of Lexington and Concord in Massachusetts. The gunpowder they took at New Castle was used at the Battle of Bunker Hill.

Six months before the Declaration of Independence was signed, New Hampshire adopted a constitution. It was the first colony to set up its own government.

After the war the U.S. Constitution was written. The new Constitution was just a piece of paper until nine of the 13 states agreed to it. When New Hampshire became the ninth state to accept the Constitution, the United States of America was really born.

New Hampshire has mountains and lakes and the shortest coastline of any state that touches an ocean. People ski and hike, swim, fish, and hunt in this state. Many people visit in the fall just to see the red, orange, and yellow leaves bright against the dark evergreens. As they drive along they can see old homes and churches and many covered bridges.

Other things to see:

Franklin Pierce Homestead — childhood home of our 14th President, at Hillsboro

Mount Washington — highest mountain in the northeast; 1869 cog railway, first in North America

Old Man of the Mountains — 40-foot-high profile (more than 12 meters) of a man's face formed by five stone ledges

Strawbery Banke — first settled in 1630; many old buildings — one is almost 300 years old, at Portsmouth

Main Products

Agriculture: fruit, hay, maple syrup, milk, plants, vegetables, wood. Forests cover almost all of New Hampshire.

Fishing: cod, lobster, pollock, shrimp.

Mining: clay, sand and gravel, stone. New Hampshire has large granite quarries.

Manufacturing: electric and electronic equipment, instruments, lumber and wood products, machinery, metal and metal products, paper and paper products, printed materials, rubber and plastic products.

New Jersey NJ

3rd State / December 18, 1787

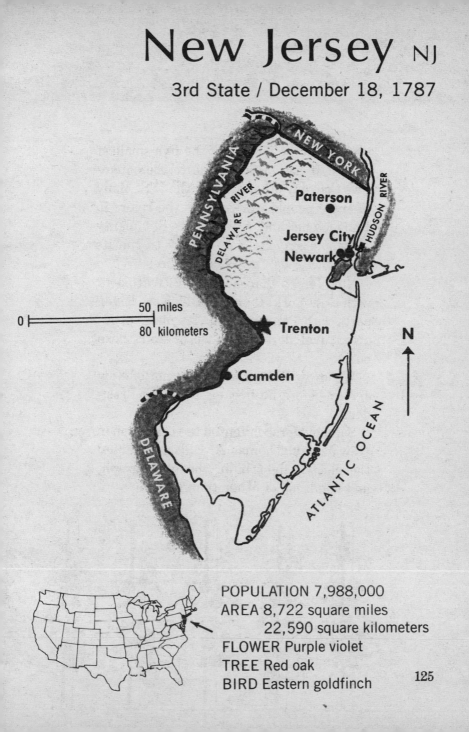

POPULATION 7,988,000
AREA 8,722 square miles
    22,590 square kilometers
FLOWER Purple violet
TREE Red oak
BIRD Eastern goldfinch

125

◆ New Jersey is one of the five smallest states. It has more people to the square mile than any other state in the U.S. Many of these people work across the rivers in Philadelphia and New York. But plenty of people stay in New Jersey to run its many factories, farms, and offices.

New Jersey shares Hudson River ports with New York. It shares Delaware River ports with Pennsylvania. Its many products travel all over the world from these ports.

Woodrow Wilson was Governor of New Jersey before he became our 28th President.

Samuel Morse invented the telegraph in New Jersey. Thomas A. Edison invented the electric light bulb, the phonograph, and hundreds of other things there.

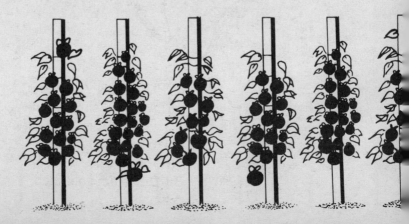

Almost 100 battles of our War of Independence were fought in New Jersey. Even so, many buildings from that time still stand.

Other things to see:

Batsto — colonial village

Beaches — along the Atlantic coast

Grover Cleveland Birthplace — our 22nd and 24th President, at Caldwell

Morristown National Historical Park — General George Washington's headquarters during the winter of 1779-1780; Fort Nonsense, museum

Thomas A. Edison National Historic Site — home and workshop, original models of many inventions

Washington Crossing — where General Washington and his men crossed the Delaware River on Christmas night, 1776, to surprise the British Army at Trenton

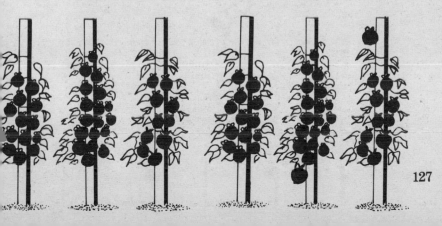

127

Main Products

Agriculture: flowers and shrubs, fruit, grain, sod, vegetables. New Jersey is a leader in tomatoes. Its farms help feed millions of people in the nearby cities of Philadelphia and New York. Less than one acre out of every five acres of New Jersey land is used for farms.

Fishing: bluefish, clams, crabs, flounder, lobster, porgy, weakfish.

Mining: sand and gravel, stone.

Manufacturing: chemicals, electric and electronic equipment, food processing, instruments, machinery, metal products, petroleum products, printing and publishing, rubber and plastic products. New Jersey is a leader in chemicals and medicines.

New Mexico NM

47th State / January 6, 1912

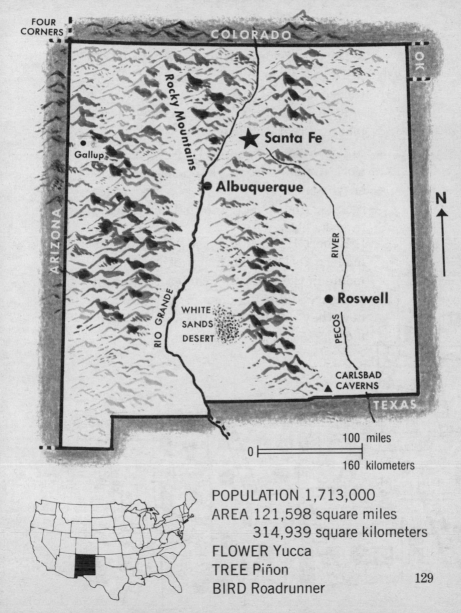

FOUR CORNERS

COLORADO

OK

Rocky Mountains

Gallup

★ Santa Fe

● Albuquerque

ARIZONA

N

RIVER

● Roswell

RIO GRANDE

WHITE SANDS DESERT

PECOS

CARLSBAD CAVERNS

TEXAS

```
        100  miles
0 ├─────────────┤
        160  kilometers
```

POPULATION 1,713,000
AREA 121,598 square miles
        314,939 square kilometers
FLOWER Yucca
TREE Piñon
BIRD Roadrunner

129

◆The world's first atomic bomb was set off in New Mexico in 1945. The bomb's heat turned sand into glass. That bomb was built in New Mexico too, in a very secret place called Los Alamos.

Today many people in New Mexico work to find more ways to use atomic energy. Some try to use it to power space rockets. And some try to find better ways to make electricity.

Robert H. Goddard, the "father of the modern rocket," did many of his experiments in the New Mexico desert. Rocket tests are still being done in the state, but now they are done by the U.S. government.

New Mexico has many pueblos. These are Indian cliff or hilltop houses that are built together like apartments. Pueblo Bonito has 600 rooms. Indians still live in some pueblos.

Indian ceremonies can be seen in many places in New Mexico. Many towns have rodeos every year.

Other things to see:

Carlsbad Caverns National Park — huge caves, mass flights of bats

Palace of the Governors — oldest public building (1610) in the U.S., in Santa Fe

Sandia Peak Tramway — longest in North America, at Albuquerque

Valley of Fires State Park — 1,500-year-old black lava flow, near Carrizozo

White Sands National Monument — desert of gypsum sand

Main Products

Agriculture: apples, beef cattle, cotton, grain, hay, lettuce, milk, peanuts, pecans, peppers, potatoes. Water is scarce in New Mexico. Most of the farming is done around the southern Rio Grande River. A lot of New Mexico's land is owned by the U.S. government.

Mining: coal, copper, natural gas, petroleum, potash, sand and gravel, uranium. New Mexico is first in potash and second in pumice. It is third in copper, and a leader in carbon dioxide.

Manufacturing: electric and electronic equipment, food processing, lumber and wood products.

New York NY

11th State / July 26, 1788

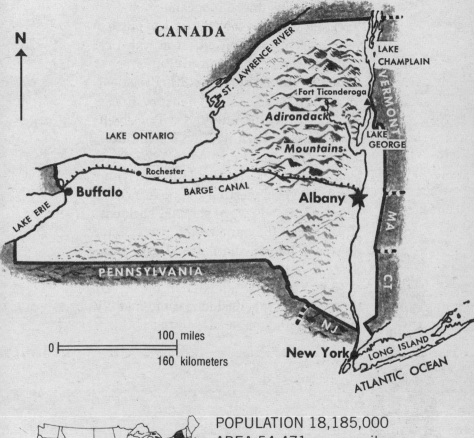

POPULATION 18,185,000
AREA 54,471 square miles
    141,080 square kilometers
FLOWER Rose
TREE Sugar maple
BIRD Bluebird

◆George Washington became our first President when he took his oath of office in New York City. The city was the first capital of the young United States.

Martin Van Buren, our 8th President; Millard Fillmore, 13th; Theodore Roosevelt, 26th; and Franklin D. Roosevelt, 32nd, were all born in New York State.

The Erie Canal opened in 1825. It ran from Lake Erie to the Hudson River. People traveled west on the canal to settle new land. Goods were shipped back east. Mules pulled the barges both ways. Today there is a bigger and better Barge Canal System.

New York is the leader in music, art, theater, banking, fashion, radio and TV, and books and magazines in the U.S.

New York City is the biggest city in the U.S. People from all over the world come to see it. Some of them visit New York State's mountains, seashore, and old buildings too.

Other things to see:

Baseball Hall of Fame — at Cooperstown

Corning Glass Center — see glass made, at Corning

Fort Ticonderoga — read about it in Vermont, page 186

Howe Caverns — largest caves in northeast U.S.

New York City — American Museum of Natural History, Bronx Zoo, Ellis Island, Empire State Building, Hayden Planetarium, Statue of Liberty, United Nations Headquarters

Niagara Falls — waterfalls shared by U.S. and Canada

Saratoga National Historical Park — where Americans beat the British in one of the most important battles of our War of Independence, near Schuylerville

U.S. Military Academy — where army officers train, at West Point

Main Products

Agriculture: beef cattle, corn, eggs, flowers and plants, fruit, milk, poultry, vegetables. New York is a leader in milk, vegetables, apples, grapes, pears, strawberries, and maple syrup.

Fishing: bluefish, clams, crabs, flounder, hake, lobster, quahogs, scup.

Mining: clays, salt, sand and gravel, stone, zinc. New York is a leader in garnets, talc, and zinc.

Manufacturing: chemicals; clothing; electric and electronic equipment; food processing; instruments; machinery; metals and metal products; paper products; photographic equipment; printing and publishing; stone, clay, and glass products; transportation equipment. New York is first in book publishing, furs, dolls and stuffed toys, instruments, and jewelry. It is a leader in many other products. New York is third in total manufacturing in the U.S.

North Carolina NC

12th State / November 21, 1789

POPULATION 7,323,000
AREA 53,821 square miles
    139,397 square kilometers
FLOWER Dogwood
TREE Pine
BIRD Cardinal

◆North Carolina was the first colony to fight its English governor. About 100 years before our War of Independence some colonists along the coast did not like the taxes on their trade with other colonies. They put their governor in jail in 1677, and ran the colony themselves until a new governor showed up in 1683.

North Carolina was the first colony to tell its delegates to the Continental Congress to vote for independence from England. After the war, the state at first did not accept the Constitution. People were afraid of having too strong a government. Under North Carolina's own constitution, they had a bill of rights to protect them. Then leaders agreed to add the Bill of Rights to the U.S. Constitution. So North Carolina voted to become a state too.

Two national seashores are on the Atlantic Ocean sandbars of North Carolina. Old shipwrecks, sand dunes, the tallest lighthouse in the U.S., swimming, fishing, and hunting — all are found there. Kitty Hawk, where the Wright brothers flew the world's first successful airplane, is on a sandbar too.

Other things to see:

Andrew Johnson Birthplace — 17th President, at Raleigh

Blue Ridge Parkway Drive — through the highest mountains in the eastern U.S.; see beautiful wild gardens in spring

Fort Raleigh National Historic Site — on Roanoke Island, home of the "Lost Colony" that was started 35 years before the Pilgrims landed; no one knows what happened to the colonists

James K. Polk Birthplace — our 11th President, at Pineville

Ocracoke Island — hideout of the pirate Blackbeard

Old Salem — colonial village, at Winston-Salem

Main Products

Agriculture: chickens, corn, eggs, greenhouse and nursery products, hogs, milk, peanuts, soybeans, tobacco, turkeys, wood. North Carolina is first in turkeys. More than half the state is covered with forests.

Fishing: clams, crabs, flounder, shrimp.

Mining: clays, gemstones, feldspar, mica, phosphate, sand and gravel, stone. North Carolina is first in feldspar and mica and second in phosphate.

Manufacturing: chemicals, electric and electronic equipment, food processing, furniture, machinery, medicines, rubber and plastic products, textiles, tobacco products. North Carolina is first in cigarettes, textiles, and wooden furniture. The world's largest denim mill is at Greensboro.

North Dakota ND

39th State / November 2, 1889

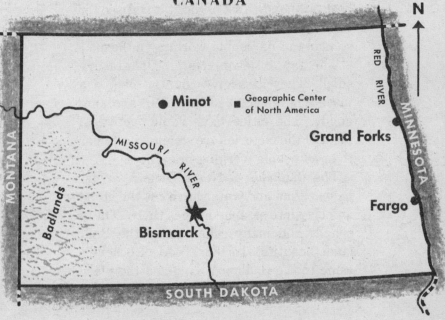

CANADA

N

Minot ● ■ Geographic Center of North America

RED RIVER

MINNESOTA

Grand Forks ●

MISSOURI RIVER

MONTANA

Badlands

Bismarck ★

Fargo ●

SOUTH DAKOTA

100 miles
0
160 kilometers

POPULATION 644,000
AREA 70,704 square miles
          183,123 square kilometers
FLOWER Wild prairie rose
TREE American elm
BIRD Western meadowlark

◆North Dakota has some of the world's best farmland. Most of the state is used for farming and ranching. No other state has so many of its people working on farms.

The few cities in North Dakota are small. The cities give country people a place where they can buy, sell, and ship goods. The cities have some factories. Most of the factories are small, with fewer than 50 people working in each.

The Badlands of North Dakota are famous. Wind and water have cut the stone and clay into strange shapes there. These shapes and many colors make the Badlands beautiful. In 1884 Teddy Roosevelt came to the Badlands. He liked the place so much he stayed two years.

North Dakota has rodeos, Indian pow-wows, fishing, boating, and horseback riding. In the winter, cross-country skiing and ice-fishing are fun. And for hunters there is lots of game.

Other things to see:

Bonanzaville — pioneer village, near Fargo

Fort Abercrombie — first army post in North Dakota

Fort Lincoln State Park — earth-lodge Indian village and reconstructed Custer home, near Mandan

Fort Union National Historic Site — full-size copy of John Jacob Astor's 1829 fur-trading post, near Williston

Geographic Center of North America — near Rugby

International Peace Garden — shared with Canada

Theodore Roosevelt National Park — prairie dogs, buffalo, deer, petrified forest, all in the Badlands where Roosevelt hunted and raised cattle

Main Products

Agriculture: barley, beans, beef cattle, flaxseed, hay, honey, milk, oats, potatoes, sunflowers, sugar beets, wheat. North Dakota is first in durum, spring wheat, and sunflower seeds. It is a leader in rye, barley, and flaxseed. Agriculture is by far North Dakota's most important business.

Mining: coal, natural gas, petroleum, sand and gravel. North Dakota has a lot of coal that is still in the ground. Coal still in the ground is called "coal reserves." North Dakota has large oil — or petroleum — reserves too.

Manufacturing: food processing, machinery, printed materials. North Dakota is a leader in machinery. The state has factories that turn coal into natural gas and corn into a gasoline additive.

Ohio OH

17th State / March 1, 1803

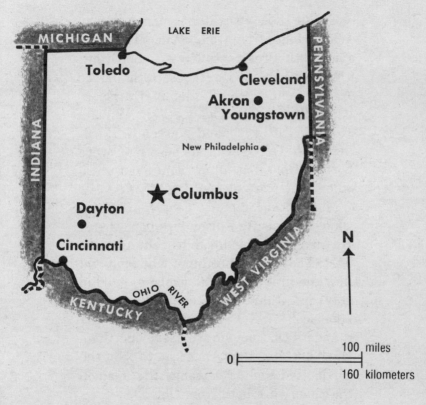

POPULATION 11,173,000
AREA 44,828 square miles
116,103 square kilometers
FLOWER Scarlet carnation
TREE Buckeye
BIRD Cardinal

◆Eight U.S. Presidents came to the White House from Ohio—William H. Harrison, 9th President; Ulysses S. Grant, 18th; Rutherford B. Hayes, 19th; James A. Garfield, 20th; Benjamin Harrison, 23rd; William McKinley, 25th; William Howard Taft, 27th; and Warren G. Harding, 29th. Only seven of these men were born in Ohio, but all of them lived there when they were elected President.

Many other famous people are from Ohio. Thomas A. Edison was born there. He invented the incandescent electric light. The Wright brothers, who built and flew the first successful airplane, lived in Dayton. John D. Rockefeller, Sr., America's first billionaire, started the Standard Oil Company in Cleveland. John H. Glenn, Jr.—first American to orbit the earth—and Neil Armstrong—first man on the moon—are both from Ohio.

Ohio is a crossroads. Pioneers traveled west on the Ohio River and Lake Erie. Later steamboats carried goods on the river and the lake. Now trains, planes, trucks, and cars crisscross the state. Boats carry products to ports near and far.

Many Ohio people work in factories. They make Ohio first in many different products — from brushes and glues to paint, toys, and children's vehicles.

Other things to see:

Adena State Memorial — 1807 stone house, 1700's and early 1800's furniture, in Chillicothe

Gardens of Zoar — 1817 settlement where men and women had equal rights, near New Philadelphia

Professional Football Hall of Fame — at Canton

Schoenbrunn Village — 1772 Christian Indian settlement, near New Philadelphia

Main Products

Agriculture: apples, beef cattle, corn, eggs, hay, hogs, milk, poultry, sheep, soybeans, vegetables, wheat, wool. Ohio is second in eggs and a leader in corn, hogs, winter wheat, and tomatoes.

Fishing: catfish, smelt, white bass, white perch, yellow perch. Pollution in Lake Erie killed many fish, but Ohio has cleaned up the lake to bring fish back. A lot of trout are raised for market.

Mining: clay and shale, coal, limestone, natural gas, petroleum, salt, sand and gravel, stone. Ohio is a leader in limestone, lime, salt, and sand and gravel.

Manufacturing: electric and electronic equipment; food processing; machinery; metals and metal products; paper products; rubber and plastic products; stone, clay, and glass products; transportation equipment. Ohio is first in machine tools, soap, and plastic products, and a leader in iron and steel, truck bodies, motorcycles, clay and glass products, Swiss cheese, and ice cream.

Oklahoma OK

46th State / November 16, 1907

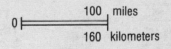

N

0 ⊢————⊣ 100 miles
⊢————⊣ 160 kilometers

POPULATION 3,301,000
AREA 69,903 square miles
      181,049 square kilometers
FLOWER Mistletoe
TREE Redbud
BIRD Scissor-tailed flycatcher

149

◆From 1820 to 1840 five Indian tribes were forced to move out of the southern states. They were given most of present-day Oklahoma in return for the land they left. Each tribe became a nation and had its own government and schools.

The state's name comes from the Choctaw Indian words "okla," for "people," and "humma," for "red."

More than half the people in the state live in cities. Oklahoma City is on top of oil fields.

Millions of people come to Oklahoma every year to visit its 200 man-made and 100 natural lakes. They can see rodeos and Indian powwows and, in watermelon season, the World's Championship Watermelon Seed Spitting Contest.

Other things to see:

Indian City — villages of seven different tribes of Plains Indians, dances, near Anadarko

Museum of the Western Prairie — pioneer life, at Altus

Tsa-La-Gi — Cherokee village, crafts and games, near Tahlequah

Wichita Mountains Wildlife Refuge — longhorn cattle and buffalo herds, prairie-dog town, near Cache

Main Products

Agriculture: beef cattle, cotton, hay, hogs, milk, peanuts, poultry, sorghum, wheat, wood. Oklahoma is a leader in wheat and cattle.

Mining: coal, gypsum, helium, iodine, natural gas, petroleum, stone. Oklahoma is a leader in natural gas, petroleum, and helium.

Manufacturing: electric machinery and equipment, food processing, machinery, metal products, petroleum and coal products, rubber and plastic products, transportation equipment. Tulsa is called the "Oil Capital of the World." That's because so many companies that do some kind of oil business have their headquarters there.

Oregon OR

33rd State / February 14, 1859

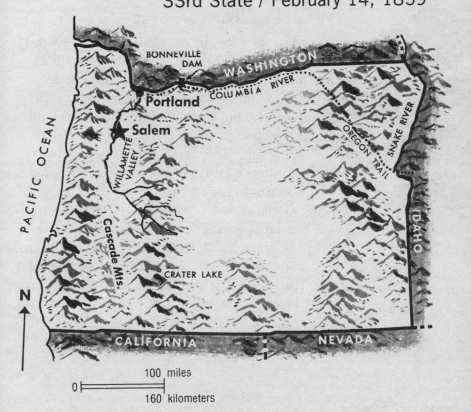

POPULATION 3,204,000
AREA 98,386 square miles
254,819 square kilometers
FLOWER Oregon grape
TREE Douglas fir
BIRD Western meadowlark

◆ When the first settlers came to Oregon, they could not get down the Columbia River. Rocks and fast water upset their boats, and some people drowned.

Now large dams have been built. The river is calm. Ocean-going ships travel up the river to where those early travelers got stuck. The same dams make power for homes and factories in Oregon and Washington.

Oregon has passed many laws to keep its land, water, and air clean. Today no one may build very close to the water along the beautiful Pacific Coast. That means all the people can enjoy the sand dunes, cliffs, and beaches.

More than 12 million people visit Oregon each year. They come to see the beautiful mountains and valleys, forests and beaches. They hunt, fish, and ski. In June some try for the Sand Castle Building championship that is held on Cannon Beach. Visitors drive along the Columbia River Gorge, past Bonneville Dam and 620-foot (186-meter) Multnomah Falls. In season, they watch salmon jump fish ladders to reach their home streams and lay their eggs.

Other things to see:

Crater Lake National Park — deepest lake in the U.S.

Fort Clatsop National Memorial — 1805-6 winter camp of Lewis and Clark expedition

Oregon Caves National Monument — guided tours

Sea Lion Caves — home of hundreds of sea lions, near Florence

Main Products

Agriculture: beef cattle; bulbs, shrubs, and seedlings; hay; milk; vegetables; wheat; wood. Almost half of Oregon is covered by forests. The state is first in azaleas, peppermint oil, blackberries, filbert nuts, and raspberries. More than half of Oregon is owned by the U.S. government.

Fishing: crabs, rock fish, salmon, shrimp, tuna.

Mining: diatomite, pumice, sand and gravel, stone. Oregon is the only state that mines nickel and Oregon sunstone, a gemstone used in jewelry.

Manufacturing: electronic equipment, food processing, lumber and wood products, paper products. Oregon is first in lumber and plywood.
Visitors are important to Oregon.

Pennsylvania PA

2nd State / December 12, 1787

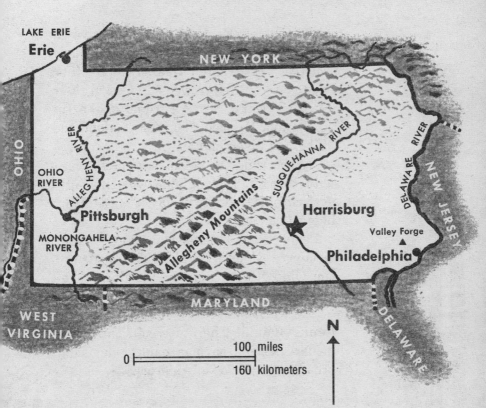

POPULATION 12,056,000
AREA 46,058 square miles
      119,291 square kilometers
FLOWER Mountain laurel
TREE Hemlock
BIRD Ruffed grouse

◆ The king of England gave Pennsylvania to William Penn in 1681. Penn was a Quaker. He wanted Quakers and other people to be free to worship God in their own ways. Penn was a friend of the Indians too. He paid them for the land the king had given him.

By the time the colonies went to war with Britain, Philadelphia was the biggest city in America. Today it is the fifth biggest city in the U.S.

Pennsylvania has important ports on the Delaware River and Lake Erie. Boats on the Ohio River carry goods down the Mississippi to New Orleans.

The world's first oil well was drilled in Pennsylvania. The state had the first medical school, savings bank, television broadcast, and zoo in America.

Independence Hall in Philadelphia could be called the birthplace of the United States. The Declaration of Independence was signed there. Our Constitution was written there too.

Philadelphia was the capital of the colonies during most of our War of Independence. Later it was the capital of the young U.S. from 1790 to 1800.

Other things to see:

Fort Ligonier — 1758 fort and equipment

Franklin Institute — hands-on science and technology, at Philadelphia

Hopewell Furnace National Historic Site — 1830's iron-making furnace and buildings, near Reading

Landis Valley/Pennsylvania Farm Museum — German rural life, 22 buildings on 40 acres, near Lancaster

Roadside America — panorama of life in rural U.S. during 200 plus years, near Hamburg

Valley Forge National Historical Park — where General Washington and his troops spent the bitter winter of 1777-78

Washington Crossing — where General Washington and his troops crossed the Delaware River to take Trenton

Wheatland — home of James Buchanan, our 15th President, at Lancaster

Main Products

Agriculture: beef cattle, corn, eggs, hay, milk, mushrooms. Pennsylvania is first in mushrooms. Much of Pennsylvania's corn and hay is used to feed its beef and dairy cattle.

Mining: coal, limestone, natural gas, petroleum, sand and gravel, stone. Pennsylvania mines nearly all the hard coal in the U.S. It is a leader in soft coal and limestone. The state is fourth in overall coal production.

Manufacturing: chemicals, clothing, electrical equipment, food processing, machinery, metal products, printed materials, transportation equipment. Pennsylvania is first in canned mushrooms. It is a leader in ice cream, steel, paper products, glass products, clothing and textiles, potato chips, and pretzels.

Rhode Island RI

13th State / May 29, 1790

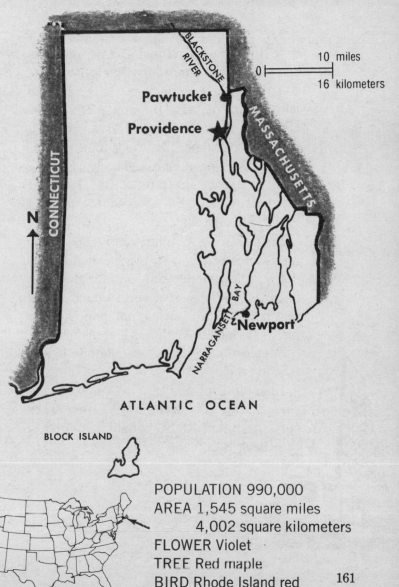

POPULATION 990,000
AREA 1,545 square miles
4,002 square kilometers
FLOWER Violet
TREE Red maple
BIRD Rhode Island red

161

◆ In 1636 a man named Roger Williams ran away from the angry Puritans in the colony of Massachusetts. He stayed all winter with friendly Indians in Rhode Island. The Puritans wanted to punish Williams. They did not like the things he said. He said the king of England had no right to give away the Indians' land. He said everyone should be allowed to worship God in his own way.

In the spring Williams and some other men started their own town called Providence. They tried to buy land for the town from the Indians. But the Indians would only take friendly gifts — not money. They gave that land to Williams and his friends.

People of many religions came to live in Rhode Island.

Rhode Island was the last colony to become a state. It waited until people were sure the Bill of Rights would be added to the Constitution.

Rhode Island is not an island at all. It is made up of 36 islands and a mainland that is almost cut in two by Narragansett Bay. Sailing and deep-sea fishing are good there. This state has many old homes, churches, and other buildings. Some are about 300 years old.

Other things to see:

Green Animals Topiary Gardens — 80 trees and shrubs cut in the shapes of animals, near Portsmouth

Newport — beautiful old houses and places of worship; Old Stone Mill that may have been built by Vikings

Old State House — independence from Great Britain claimed on May 4, 1776, two months before the Continental Congress's Declaration of Independence, at Providence

Slater Mill Historic Site — 1793 yarn mill called the "Cradle of American Industry," hand spinning, weaving, early textile machines, at Pawtucket

163

Main Products

Agriculture: apples, chickens, eggs, potatoes, trees and shrubs, and turf grass.

Fishing: clams, flounder, lobsters, quahogs

Mining: sand and gravel, stone

Manufacturing: electric and electronic equipment, jewelry, machinery, metal and metal products, textiles. Rhode Island is a leader in jewelry and silverware.

South Carolina SC

8th State / May 23, 1788

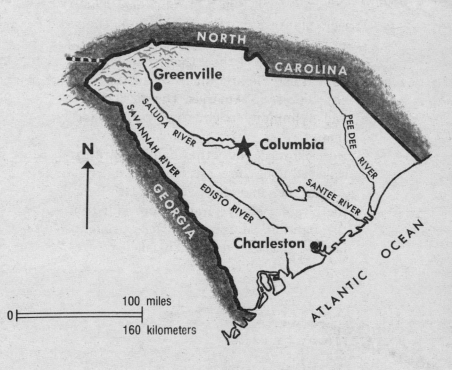

100 miles

0

160 kilometers

POPULATION 3,699,000
AREA 32,008 square miles
     82,901 square kilometers
FLOWER Yellow jessamine
TREE Palmetto
BIRD Carolina wren

◆ As a colony, South Carolina had many rich plantations. People brought their crops and furs to the city of Charleston. The city was a big port then — just as it is now. It had the first museum and the first real theater in America. Our first opera and symphony orchestra were heard there.

Blackbeard and other famous pirates sailed all along the coast. No ship was safe. At last men and ships were sent to fight the pirates. Many pirates were killed in the fighting. Many more were brought back to Charleston and hanged.

Many battles — large and small — in our War of Independence took place in South Carolina. Some were fought by regular American soldiers and militiamen. Others were fought by American guerrillas who lived in the swamps. Many places where battles were fought can still be seen in the state.

Other things to see:

Andrew Jackson State Park — birthplace of our 7th President, near Lancaster

Gardens — South Carolina is famous for its beautiful gardens; several are near Charleston

George Washington portrait — before false teeth changed the shape of his face, and without his wig, Charleston City Hall

Venus flytrap — insect-trapping plant that grows wild in U.S. only in North and South Carolina

Woodrow Wilson's Boyhood Home — our 28th President, in Columbia

Main Products

Agriculture: beef cattle, chickens, corn, cotton, eggs, fruit, hogs, milk, soybeans, tobacco, vegetables, wood. South Carolina is a leader in peaches and tobacco. More than half the state is covered with forests.

Fishing: clams, crabs, crayfish, grouper, oysters, shrimp, snapper, swordfish, wreckfish.

Mining: clays, gold, sand and gravel, stone, vermiculite. South Carolina is a leader in kaolin and vermiculite.

Manufacturing: chemicals, clothing, electrical equipment, metal products, machinery, paper products, rubber and plastic products, textiles. Some chemicals are used for man-made fibers. Many of these fibers are woven into textiles. South Carolina is a leader in textiles.

South Dakota SD

40th State / November 2, 1889

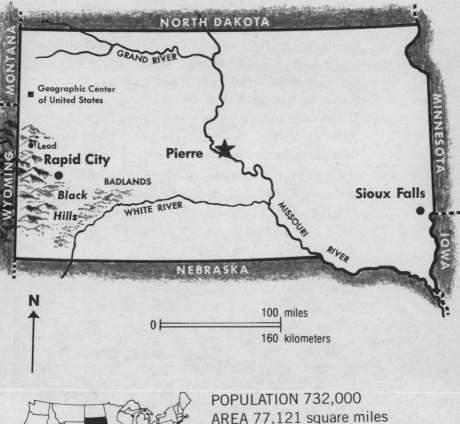

N

100 miles

0 |⊢⊢⊢⊢⊢|

160 kilometers

POPULATION 732,000
AREA 77,121 square miles
　　　199,745 square kilometers
FLOWER Pasqueflower
TREE Black Hills spruce
BIRD Ring-necked pheasant

169

◆South Dakota is an important farm state. Cattle and sheep are raised on the plains in the western part of the state. Some cattle are sent to eastern South Dakota to be fattened for market. Dairy cattle, hogs, and most of the field crops are raised in eastern South Dakota.

Four very large dams were built on the Missouri River in South Dakota. They form large lakes for people to enjoy. They make power for homes and factories. They also collect water. Farmers use that water to irrigate land in the western part of the state. Now some crops can be grown in western South Dakota.

Sports, Indians, frontier life, ghost towns, huge statues, and beautiful country bring millions of visitors to South Dakota each year.

Other things to see:

Badlands National Park — beautiful colored rocks in strange shapes

Black Hills National Forest — shared with Wyoming

Crazy Horse Memorial — statue of Sioux chief carved on mountain, near Custer

Dinosaur Park — life-size cement dinosaurs, Rapid City

1880 train — ride it in the famous Black Hills

Geographic Center of U.S. — near Castle Rock

Jewel Cave National Monument — beautiful crystals

Lead — largest working gold mine in America

Mount Rushmore National Memorial — heads of four Presidents, each about six stories high, carved in side of stone mountain

Main Products

Agriculture: beef cattle, corn, eggs, flaxseed, hay, hogs, milk, oats, rye, sheep, soybeans, sunflowers, wheat, wool. Almost all of South Dakota is used for farms and ranches. The state is a leader in sheep, cattle, hogs, alfalfa seed, barley, flaxseed, hay, oats, rye, sunflowers, and wool. Agriculture is the state's most important business.

Mining: clay, gold, sand and gravel, stone. South Dakota is a leader in gold.

Manufacturing: electric and electronic equipment, food processing, lumber, machinery, printing and publishing, stone and clay products. Most of South Dakota's factories are small. They have fewer than 50 people working in each.

Tennessee TN

16th State / June 1, 1796

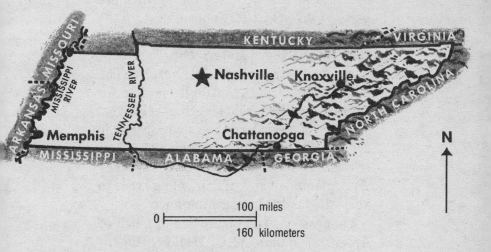

POPULATION 5,320,000
AREA 42,146 square miles
109,158 square kilometers
FLOWER Iris
TREE Tulip poplar
BIRD Mockingbird

◆ For years the trees in the Tennessee River Valley were cut down. Rains washed the loose topsoil away. Farmers could not grow crops. Floods came often.

The Tennessee River Valley includes parts of seven states. Congress set up the Tennessee Valley Authority (TVA) in 1933 to help these states. The TVA built dams to control the flood waters. The dams and their locks made it possible for ships to use the whole length of the river. The dams formed large lakes where people swim, boat, and fish. And they make electric power for homes and factories. The TVA planted over a billion young trees to keep the land from washing away.

Tennessee is the birthplace of much of America's music. W.C. Handy, the so-called Father of the Blues, lived in Memphis. And Nashville is the home of country and western music.

Three U.S. Presidents came from Tennessee. Their homes can still be seen. Andrew Jackson, 7th President, lived at The Hermitage, near Nashville. James K. Polk, 11th President, lived in Columbia. Andrew Johnson, 17th President, had a home and a tailor shop in Greenville.

Davy Crockett was born near Limestone, Tennessee. You can see his birthplace and three other places where he lived — one in Morristown, one near Lawrenceburg, and one in Rutherford.

Other things to see:

Cades Cove — see how people lived in pioneer days, in Great Smoky Mountain National Park

"Casey" Jones Home and Railroad Museum—in Jackson

Grand Ole Opry — in Nashville

Lookout Mountain — ride the world's steepest passenger incline-railway, see five states from the top, at Chattanooga

Tennessee Walking Horse — many farms and training stables near Shelbyville

Main Products

Agriculture: cattle, chickens, corn, cotton, hay, hogs, milk, plants and shrubs, soybeans, tobacco, wood. Tennessee is a leader in cotton. The world's largest cotton market is in Memphis. Freshwater pearls are grown in the western valley of the Tennessee River.

Mining: ball clay, coal, stone, zinc. Tennessee is first in ball clay and second in zinc.

Manufacturing: chemicals, electric and electronic equipment, food processing, machinery, metal products, printed materials, rubber and plastic products, transportation equipment. Tennessee is a leader in music recording and printing and publishing.

Texas TX

28th State / December 29, 1845

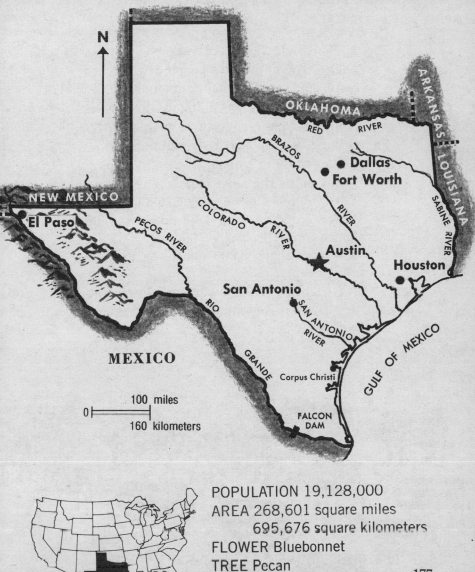

POPULATION 19,128,000
AREA 268,601 square miles
     695,676 square kilometers
FLOWER Bluebonnet
TREE Pecan
BIRD Mockingbird

177

◆ You could fit 220 Rhode Islands into Texas. The only state larger than Texas is Alaska. Texas stretches about 800 miles (1,280 kilometers) in each direction. Grapefruit can grow down near the Rio Grande. Yet up north the winters are as cold as those in Illinois.

Texas has the most farms of any state. Cattle ranches cover about two thirds of the state. More than 4,000 kinds of wild flowers grow in Texas. The city of Tyler has more than 38,000 bushes in its rose garden.

Dwight D. Eisenhower, 34th President, and Lyndon B. Johnson, 36th, were both born in Texas.

Old forts, caverns, rodeos, fairs — all these and more can be found in many parts of Texas. In San Antonio you will find the Alamo—the church where Davy Crockett, Jim Bowie, and many others died. They were fighting Mexico to free Texas.

Other things to see:

Hertzberg Circus Collection — including room-size model of a complete circus, in San Antonio

McDonald Observatory — 107-inch (268-centimeter) reflector telescope (one of the world's largest), near Fort Davis

Padre Island National Seashore — 80 miles (128 kilometers) of beaches and shifting dunes that uncover shells, arrowheads, and shipwrecks, near Corpus Christi

Prairie Dog Town—a few of the millions of prairie dogs that once lived on the plains, in Lubbock

Ysleta—town built in 1681, now part of El Paso

179

Main Products

Agriculture: beef cattle, corn, cotton, fruits, greenhouse and nursery products, hay, nuts, poultry, rice, sorghum, wheat. Texas is first in beef cattle, cotton, sheep, vegetables, and mohair and a leader in sorghum.

Fishing: black drum, crab, flounder, oysters, red snapper, red drum, sea trout, shrimp. Catfish are raised for market.

Mining: natural gas, petroleum, salt, sulfur. Texas is first in petroleum and natural gas and a leader in Frasch sulfur and salt.

Manufacturing: chemicals; electric and electronic equipment; food processing; machinery; metals and metal products; petroleum and coal products; printed materials; stone, clay, and glass products; transportation equipment.

Utah UT

45th State / January 4, 1896

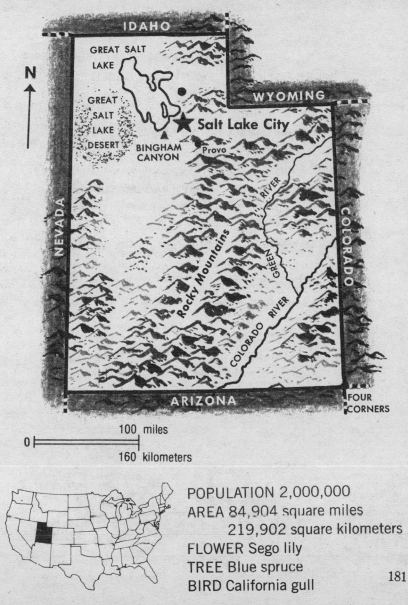

POPULATION 2,000,000
AREA 84,904 square miles
　　　219,902 square kilometers
FLOWER Sego lily
TREE Blue spruce
BIRD California gull

◆ The Mormons had to leave their old homes in Ohio, Missouri, and Illinois because some neighbors did not like their religion. Their leader, Brigham Young, looked for a place no one else would want.

In 1847 he led the Mormons to the Great Salt Lake in Utah. The land around the lake was mostly desert and mountains. The Mormons brought water to the desert and made things grow. Clouds of grasshoppers came and ate everything green. Then seagulls landed and gobbled up the grasshoppers. Enough food was saved to keep the Mormons alive until new crops could be grown.

The Mormons went out to other parts of Utah too. There they built forts and made the desert bloom. They found iron and coal and timber for all the Mormons to use.

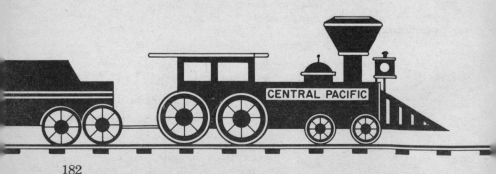

CENTRAL PACIFIC

Utah has five national parks, five national monuments, and shares two others with Colorado. Wind, sand, and water have made strange shapes out of Utah's colorful rocks. Deep canyons, caves, natural bridges, petrified forests, deserts — Utah has all these and more. Lakes, streams, mountains, and forests are playgrounds for hunting, fishing, swimming, and skiing.

Other things to see:

Arches National Park — arches, windows, and spires of red sandstone, near Moab

Cliff dwellings — built by Pueblo Indians many hundreds of years ago, in many valleys and canyons

Dinosaur National Monument — see dinosaur bones still in the ground, near Vernal

Golden Spike National Historic Site — where railroad tracks from east and west met in 1869, at Promontory

UNION PACIFIC

Main Products

Agriculture: beef cattle, eggs, fruit, hay, hogs, milk, sheep, turkeys, wheat, wool. A third of Utah is desert. If there were more water, more crops could be grown. More than half of Utah's land is owned by the U.S. government.

Mining: coal, copper, gilsonite, gold iron ore, lead, molybdenum, natural gas, petroleum, sand and gravel, uranium. Utah is a leader in gold, copper, and many other minerals.

Manufacturing: electric and electronic equipment; food processing; machinery; metals and metal products; petroleum and coal products; printing and publishing; stone, glass, and clay products; transportation equipment. The largest U.S. Swiss cheese factory is at Smithfield. Utah makes many of the replacement parts of the human body that doctors use.

Vermont VT

14th State / March 4, 1791

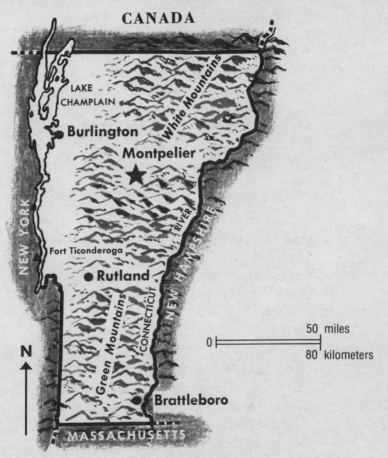

CANADA

LAKE CHAMPLAIN

White Mountains

● Burlington

Montpelier

★

NEW YORK

RIVER

Fort Ticonderoga

● Rutland

Green Mountains

CONNECTICUT

NEW HAMPSHIRE

N

Brattleboro ●

MASSACHUSETTS

0   50 miles

      80 kilometers

POPULATION 589,000
AREA 9,615 square miles
     24,903 square kilometers
FLOWER Red clover
TREE Sugar maple
BIRD Hermit thrush

◆ Both New Hampshire and New York claimed Vermont. English governors in both colonies gave away Vermont land. They gave the same land away to different people. Vermont men, led by Ethan Allen, formed a group called the Green Mountain Boys. They chased many New York settlers off the Vermont land.

By the time the War of Independence began, the Green Mountain Boys were used to working—and fighting—together. They went to New York, to the strongest fort in America—Fort Ticonderoga. And there, in May, 1775, the Green Mountain Boys took Fort Ticonderoga from the British.

Vermont fought with the American colonies against the British. But Vermont was a separate country until 1791. That's when Vermont paid New York's land claims. Then it became our 14th state—the first state after the original 13 colonies.

Vermont's first constitution was written in Old Constitution House at Windsor in 1777. It made Vermont a separate country. It said men could not own slaves. It said men did not have to own property to vote.

Other things to see:

Calvin Coolidge Historic Site — our 30th President, at Plymouth Notch

Chester Alan Arthur Historic Site — our 21st President, near Fairfield

Hyde log cabin — built in 1738, on Grand Isle

Shelburne Museum — 37 early American buildings, side-wheeler steamship, at Shelburne

Peter Matteson Tavern — 200-year-old stagecoach tavern, at Shaftsbury

Green Mountain Railroad — 26-mile scenic train ride, at Bellows Falls

Main Products

Agriculture: apples, beef cattle, cheese, eggs, hay, maple sugar and syrup, milk, wood. Forests cover much more than half the state.

Mining: sand and gravel, stone. Vermont is a leader in granite, slate, and talc.

Manufacturing: electric and electronic equipment, food processing, measuring instruments, lumber and wood products, machinery, metal products, paper and paper products, printed materials. Stuffed toys and quilts are made in Vermont. Visitors are very important to Vermont.

Virginia VA

10th State / June 25, 1788

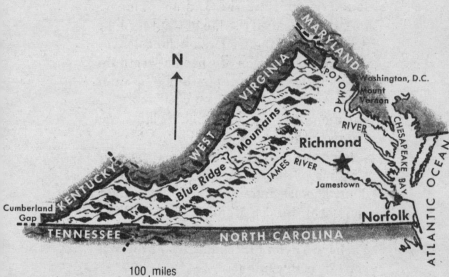

POPULATION 6,675,000
AREA 42,777 square miles
    110,792 square kilometers
FLOWER Flowering dogwood
TREE Dogwood tree
BIRD Cardinal

◆ Colonists landed at Jamestown, Virginia, in 1607. They started the first successful English colony in America. There is a legend that the Indian princess Pocahontas saved the life of Captain John Smith, one of the leaders of the colony.

Thomas Jefferson of Virginia wrote the Declaration of Independence. James Madison of Virginia helped write our Constitution. And Virginia's bill of rights was the model for the U.S. Bill of Rights.

Eight U.S. Presidents were born in Virginia: George Washington, 1st President; Thomas Jefferson, 3rd; James Madison, 4th; James Monroe, 5th; William Henry Harrison, 9th; John Tyler, 10th; Zachary Taylor, 12th; and Woodrow Wilson, 28th President.

Millions of people come to Virginia every year to see the many places that are so important in the history of the U.S. Many enjoy the mountains, caves, and fishing too.

Other things to see:

Chesapeake Bay Bridge-Tunnel — 17.6 miles (28 kilometers) of tunnels, bridges, and man-made islands

Jamestown — full-size copies of 1607 fort and ships

Monticello — home of Thomas Jefferson

Mount Vernon — home of George Washington

Norfolk Naval Station and Naval Air Station — world's largest, with ships, submarines, and jet planes

Wild pony round-up — once a year on Assateague Island

Williamsburg — more than 80 homes, public buildings, and shops that are at least 200 years old; crafts

Yorktown — where the English surrendered to George Washington

Main Products

Agriculture: apples, beef cattle, chickens, corn, cotton, eggs, hogs, milk, peanuts, soybeans, tobacco, tomatoes, turkeys, wood. Virginia is a leader in turkeys and apples. Forests cover more than half the state.

Fishing: bluefish, clams, crabs, flounder, menhaden, oysters, scallops, sea trout. Virginia is first in blue crabs and fresh-shucked oysters. Farms raise trout and other fish.

Mining: coal, iron oxide, lime, sand and gravel, stone, trap rock, vermiculite.

Manufacturing: chemicals, clothing, electric and electronic equipment, food processing, furniture and fixtures, lumber and wood products, machinery, paper products, printing and publishing, textiles, tobacco products, transportation equipment. Many people in Virginia work for the U.S. government or serve in the armed forces.

Washington WA

42nd State / November 11, 1889

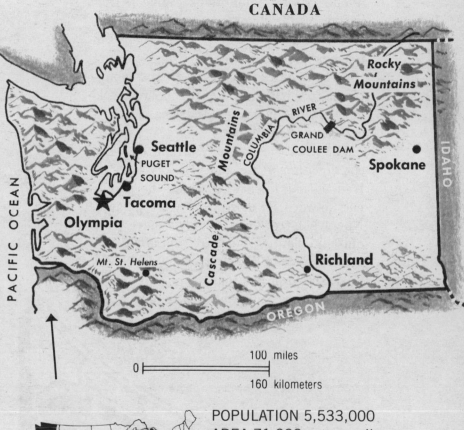

CANADA

Rocky Mountains

RIVER

COLUMBIA

Mountains

GRAND COULEE DAM

Seattle

PUGET SOUND

Spokane

Tacoma

Olympia

Cascade

Mt. St. Helens

Richland

PACIFIC OCEAN

IDAHO

OREGON

100 miles

0

160 kilometers

POPULATION 5,533,000
AREA 71,302 square miles
       184,672 square kilometers
FLOWER Coast rhododendron
TREE Western hemlock
BIRD Willow goldfinch

◆The Cascade Mountains divide Washington. Water vapor from the ocean is carried east by the wind. When the wind reaches the mountains, it drops most of the water on the west side of the mountains. So the land east of the mountains is very dry. Many farmers there have to irrigate their fields.

The great forests of Washington were cut down for years and years. When the trees near a town were gone, the people had no work. So more trees were planted. Now when trees are cut down more trees must be planted. So there will always be great forests in Washington.

Washington has many dams. It makes more power from water than any other state.

Many people come to the state of Washington to enjoy the great outdoors. Mountain climbing and skiing, hunting and fishing are favorite sports. Three national parks have been set aside in Washington's beautiful mountains. About 40 different kinds of fish are found in the Columbia and Snake rivers.

Other things to see:

Floating bridges — across Lake Washington, at Seattle

Fort Vancouver National Historic Site — 1825 fur-trading post

Ginko Petrified Forest — most different kinds of "stone" trees, near Ephrata

Grand Coulee Dam — largest concrete dam in U.S.

Monorail — ride a single-rail train, at Seattle

Puget Sound — ferryboat rides around the islands

Rocky Reach Dam — watch salmon swim upstream to lay eggs in season, near Wenatchee

U.S.S. *Turner Joy* — 418-foot destroyer that served in the Vietnam War, at Bremerton

Main Products

Agriculture: beef cattle, chickens, eggs, fruit, hay, hops, milk, potatoes, wheat, wood. Washington is first in apples, hops, pears, and sweet cherries and a leader in several other kinds of fruit, asparagus, wheat, green peas, potatoes, barley, and iris and daffodil bulbs. Forests cover almost half the state.

Fishing: clams, crab, halibut, oysters, rockfish, sablefish, salmon, sea urchins, shrimp, sole, whiting.

Mining: clays, coal, diatomite, gold, olivine, sand and gravel, stone.

Manufacturing: clothing, electric and electronic equipment, food processing, instruments, lumber and wood products, machinery, metals and metal products, paper and paper products, printed materials, software, transportation equipment. Washington is first in large passenger planes and a leader in aluminum and lumber.

West Virginia WV

35th State / June 20, 1863

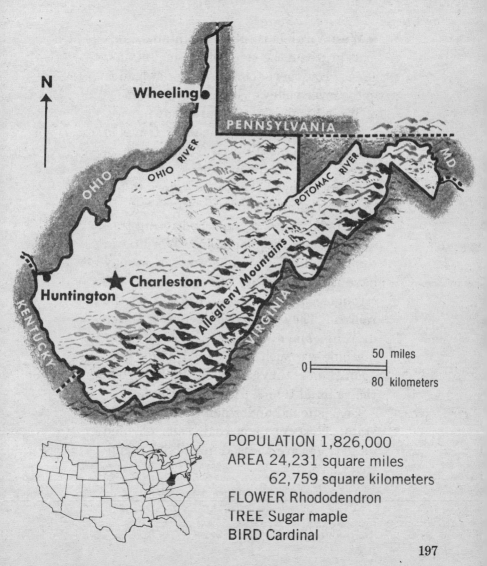

N

Wheeling

PENNSYLVANIA

OHIO RIVER

OHIO

POTOMAC RIVER

MD.

Allegheny Mountains

★ Charleston

Huntington

KENTUCKY

VIRGINIA

50 miles
0
80 kilometers

POPULATION 1,826,000
AREA 24,231 square miles
    62,759 square kilometers
FLOWER Rhododendron
TREE Sugar maple
BIRD Cardinal

◆ West Virginia is full of mountains. Animals graze on the sides of the mountains. Trees grow there too. The only flat land is in the river valleys. So that is where most of West Virginia's crops are grown.

The rough land made it hard to travel in West Virginia. Trappers and traders traveled the rivers in canoes and boats. Settlers followed trails near rivers to get through the mountains.

To build railroads men had to dig tunnels through the mountains. Working in tunnels is hard and dangerous. You may have heard the story of John Henry, the strongest man who ever worked on the railroad. They say he won a contest with a drilling machine. But beating that machine was such hard work it killed him. John Henry, they say, died right there in the railroad tunnel in West Virginia.

Coal is found under half the land in the state. West Virginia coal, salt, oil, and natural gas are all used in making chemicals there.

George Washington was 16 years old when he went to West Virginia. He went there to measure Lord Fairfax's land. The country was beautiful, and very few people lived there. Washington liked West Virginia. When he was older, he bought land there.

Many people come to West Virginia to see the beautiful mountains. They hunt and fish there. They visit caves and coal mines. They watch glass being blown. And they take canoes or rafts down fast-running streams.

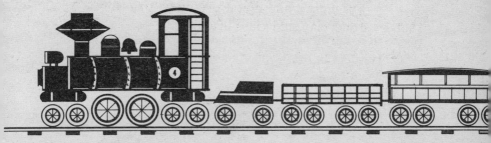

Other things to see:

Beckley Exhibition Mine — ride a coal car through an 1890's mine; old and new coal mining methods explained by miner guides, at Beckley

Cass Scenic Railroad — ride old logging train engines to the mountain top, near Cass

Watters Smith Memorial Park — pioneer farm just as it looked about 200 years ago, near Clarksburg

199

Main Products

Agriculture: chickens, corn, fruit, milk, sheep, wool. West Virginia is a leader in apples. Forests cover much more than half the state.

Mining: coal, natural gas, petroleum, sand and gravel, stone. West Virginia is a leader in coal. Some West Virginia sand is very good for making glass. Some of West Virginia's mountain spring water is bottled for sale.

Manufacturing: car parts; chemicals; clothing; lumber and wood products; machinery; metals and metal products; printing; stone, clay, and glass products.

Wisconsin WI

30th State / May 29, 1848

LAKE SUPERIOR

100 miles

0

160 kilometers

MICHIGAN

MINNESOTA

ST. CROIX RIVER

MENOMINEE RIVER

MISSISSIPPI RIVER

Green Bay

LAKE MICHIGAN

N

WISCONSIN RIVER

IOWA

Madison ★ Milwaukee

Racine

ILLINOIS

POPULATION 5,160,000
AREA 65,499 square miles
169,642 square kilometers
FLOWER Wood violet
TREE Sugar maple
BIRD Robin

◆The first white settlers in Wisconsin came to mine lead. When the lead was gone, some stayed to farm.

Men cut down Wisconsin's forests. When the trees near a town were gone, the people had no work. Lumber ghost towns were left. Some towns found new ways for people to earn a living. Now people in Wisconsin grow more trees each year than they cut down. That way they will always have forests.

The first statewide bicycle trail was set up in Wisconsin. Many laws to help the blind, old people, children, and people without jobs were passed first in Wisconsin. Later other states and the U.S. government passed laws like those in Wisconsin.

People come to Wisconsin's lakes and forests all year long. They hunt, fish, and hike. In winter, they ski, ice-boat, and ice-fish. In summer they can see a log-rolling championship.

Other things to see:

Cave of the Mounds — colored stone shapes, near Blue Mounds

Circus World Museum — old circus equipment, small summer circus, at Baraboo where the Ringling brothers began

Stonefield Village — 1890's crossroad village; old farm equipment and handcrafts, near Cassville

Wisconsin Dells — boat trip past rocks cut in strange shapes by Wisconsin River

Main Products

Agriculture: corn, eggs, hay, milk, potatoes, wood. Wisconsin is first in mink, second in milk, and a leader in cranberries, green peas, sweet corn, snap beans, and honey. Forests cover almost half the state.

Fishing: buffalo fish, catfish, chub, herring, mussels, whitefish.

Mining: sand and gravel, stone.

Manufacturing: electric and electronic equipment, food processing, lumber and wood products, machinery, metals and metal products, paper and paper products, plastic products, printed materials, transportation equipment. Wisconsin is a leader in cheese and butter, ice cream, and dried milk, as well as beer, canned vegetables, meat products, paper and small gasoline engines.

Wyoming WY

44th State / July 10, 1890

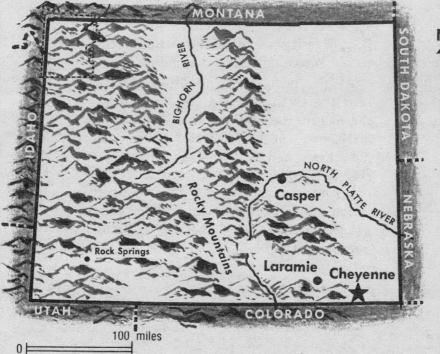

YELLOWSTONE NATIONAL PARK

MONTANA

IDAHO

SOUTH DAKOTA

N

BIGHORN RIVER

NORTH PLATTE RIVER

Casper

NEBRASKA

Rocky Mountains

Rock Springs

Laramie • Cheyenne ★

UTAH

COLORADO

100 miles

0

160 kilometers

POPULATION 481,000
AREA 97,818 square miles
253,349 square kilometers
FLOWER Indian paintbrush
TREE Cottonwood
BIRD Meadowlark

205

◆Very few people live on the plains and mountains of Wyoming. They share their state with cattle, sheep, oil wells, and millions of visitors. Most of the visitors come to see Wyoming's natural wonders.

At Yellowstone Park molten rock is near the earth's surface. The heat from the molten rock warms water from rain and snow. The heated water makes the hot springs and mud pots and geysers of this fantastic park.

Wyoming women were the first women in the U.S. to have the right to vote. They got that right in 1869 — before Wyoming became a state.

Rodeos, Indian dances, hunting, fishing, skiing, mountain climbing — beautiful Wyoming has them all.

Other things to see:

Devils Tower — first U.S. National Monument, rock columns as high as an 80-story building and shaped like tree stumps; prairie dog town, near Sundance

Fort Laramie National Historic Site — this fort that helped win the West still has 21 buildings

Grand Teton National Park — beautiful Teton mountains, glaciers, the valley called Jackson Hole, and lakes; world's largest elk herd

Hot Springs State Park — world's largest single mineral hot springs, near Thermopolis

Yellowstone — world's first National Park, largest in the lower 48 states; canyons, colored pools, geysers, hot springs, mud pots, waterfalls, wild animals

Main Products

Agriculture: barley, beef cattle, buffalo, corn, dry beans, hay, sheep, sugar beets, wheat, wood, wool. Wyoming is a leader in sheep and wool. Most of its land is used for grazing cattle and sheep. Almost half the state is owned by the U.S. government. The government decides who can graze, mine, and log on its land.

Mining: bentonite, coal, natural gas, petroleum, trona. The state has large reserves of coal. Mining is Wyoming's most important business.

Manufacturing: chemicals; lumber and wood products; petroleum and coal products; printed materials; stone, clay, and glass products.

The 13 Original States

1790

*What is now the state of Maine was owned by Massachusetts.

**What is now the state of Vermont was claimed by New Hampshire and New York.

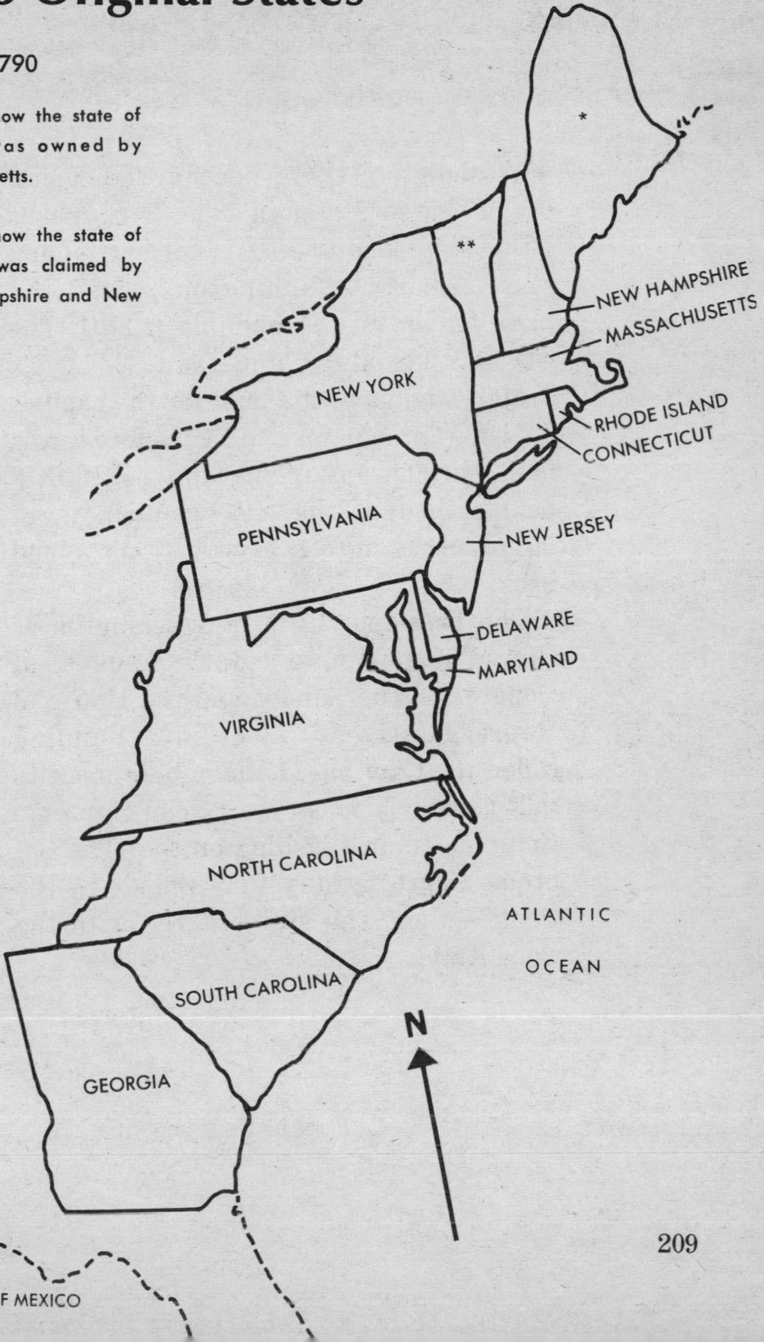

NEW HAMPSHIRE

MASSACHUSETTS

NEW YORK

RHODE ISLAND

CONNECTICUT

PENNSYLVANIA

NEW JERSEY

DELAWARE

MARYLAND

VIRGINIA

NORTH CAROLINA

ATLANTIC

OCEAN

N

SOUTH CAROLINA

GEORGIA

GULF OF MEXICO

◆Washington, D.C., became the capital of the United States in 1800. D.C. means District of Columbia. It is not part of any state. George Washington picked the place for the city to be built in 1791. The city was named for him.

Maryland gave the land for the capital. A plan was made for the city before it was built. Virginia gave some land too. In 1846 people thought the city would not get larger. So Congress gave Virginia's land back.

The President lives in Washington at the White House. Both houses of Congress — the Senate and the House of Representatives — meet in a building called the Capitol. The members meet to talk about and pass laws. The Supreme Court meets in Washington too. The Supreme Court decides if laws made by the Congress and the states agree with the Constitution.

Washington, D.C.

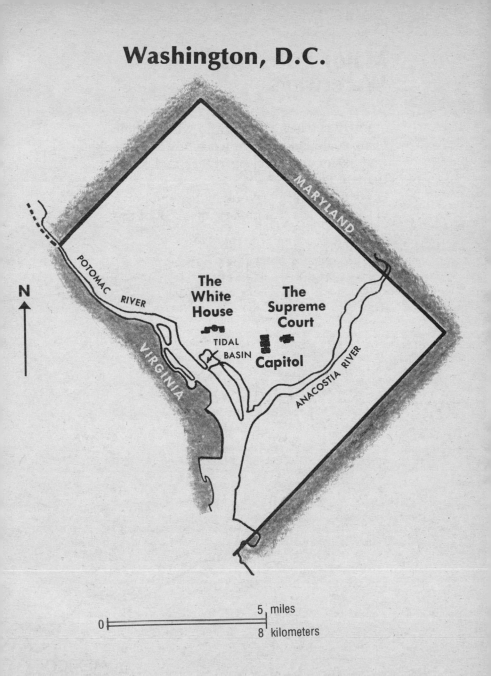

MARYLAND

POTOMAC RIVER

The White House

The Supreme Court

TIDAL BASIN

Capitol

VIRGINIA

ANACOSTIA RIVER

N

0 | 5 miles
0 | 8 kilometers

Major Ports and Waterways

Early settlers built towns where their boats could land. There were no roads. It was easier to travel on rivers and lakes than on land.

Today the large rivers, lakes, and ports of the U.S. are still important. A lot of the

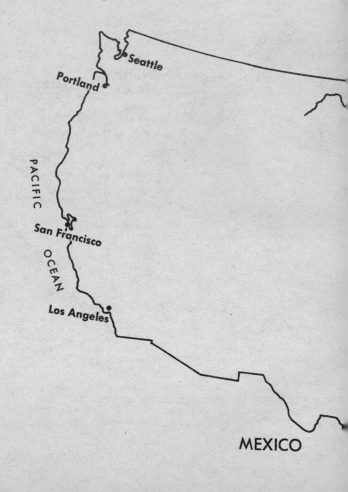

goods that the U.S. produces are shipped in boats to other parts of our country. Some are sent to other countries. And other countries send goods to us.

The Great Lakes — Erie, Huron, Michigan, Ontario, and Superior — are the largest group of freshwater lakes in the world.

Mountain Ranges

The Green Mountains, the White Mountains, the Adirondacks, the Allegheny, Blue Ridge, Cumberland, Black, and Great Smoky mountains are some of the names given to parts of the Appalachian Mountains in different states.

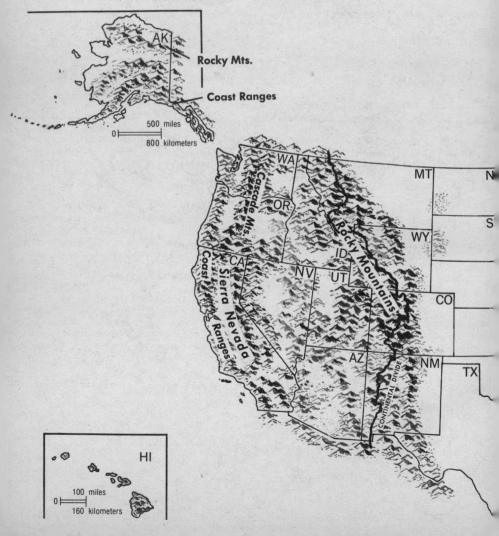

The Continental Divide lies along the highest part of the Rocky Mountains. That is where the waters divide. Some water runs down on the west side and some on the east. The waters that run west go to the Pacific Ocean. The others go to the Atlantic. Water that runs into the Gulf of Mexico ends up in the Atlantic Ocean. There are divides in other high places too. Some divides send water north and south.

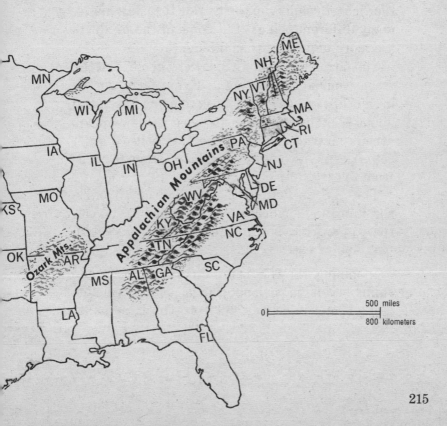

500 miles

800 kilometers

The 50 States Together

The 50 states together make the United States the richest country in the world. It makes many, many different things. But some of the products are more important than others.

The farmland in the U.S. is very good. And the farmers make the most of it. Every farm worker in the U.S. grows enough food to feed himself and about 73 other Americans, as well as 26 people in other countries. The food the U.S. sells to other countries helps pay for the many things it needs from those countries.

The U.S. is first in the world in corn, milk, sorghum, and soybeans and a leader in beef, cotton, eggs, fruit, hogs, peanuts, tobacco, vegetables, and wheat.

In mining, the U.S. is first in bromine, salt, and sulfur, second in coal, natural gas, and petroleum, and a leader in copper and iron. The U.S. makes so many things and uses so much oil that it has to buy large amounts of oil and many other minerals from other countries.

Manufacturing is very big business in the U.S. The U.S. makes more manufactured goods than any other country. It is first in aircraft, aluminum, chemicals, computer hardware and software, construction machinery, electric power, plastics, rockets, satellites, and scientific instruments and a leader in automobiles, clothing, and steel. The U.S. sells many manufactured goods to other countries too.

What other kinds of work do people do in the U.S.? They buy and sell things. They work for the government. They build homes, offices, factories, and roads. They run trains and buses and airplanes. They work in schools, banks, laundries, power stations, and other places where people need things done.

In every state some people do important jobs for the rest of the people in their state. And some people do important jobs for the rest of the people in the whole United States.

More Fabulous Facts about the Fifty States

The world's first atomic bomb was set off in New Mexico in 1945.

The oldest road in the United States is El Camino Real, built in 1581 in New Mexico.

New York City has more people than any other city in the United States.

California has more people than any other state in the United States.

The first capital of the United States was New York City.

The geographic center of North America is near Rugby, North Dakota.

The geographic center of the United States is near Castle Rock, South Dakota.

Oroville Dam in California is the highest dam in the United States.

Wyoming was the first place in the United States where women could vote.

The Great Lakes are the largest group of freshwater lakes in the world.

The wettest place in the world is Mt. Waialeale in Hawaii.

The highest paved road in the United States is Mount Evans Highway in Colorado. It rises to 14,264 feet (4,279 meters).

The deepest canyon in the U.S. is Kings Canyon in California. It is 8,200 feet (2,499 meters) deep at its deepest point.

The world's largest canyon is the Grand Canyon on the Colorado River in Arizona. It is 277 miles (446 kilometers) long and 13 miles (21 kilometers) across at its widest point and one mile (1.609 kilometers) deep.

Boulder, Colorado, is the only city in the United States to own a glacier.

More Fabulous Facts

The first whites settled in America at St. Augustine, Florida, in 1565—more than 400 years ago.

 The first passenger train in the United States ran between Augusta, Georgia, and Charleston, South Carolina, in 1834.

The first woman in the United States Senate was Rebecca Felton from Georgia. She went to the Senate in 1922.

Hawaii is the only state that grows coffee.

The world's tallest geyser is Steamboat Geyser in Wyoming.

The world's longest natural bridge is Kolob Arch in Utah.

Patrick Henry said, "Give me liberty, or give me death!" in Virginia in 1775.

The world's tallest battle monument is at Houston, Texas.

The largest standing clock in the world is the Colgate clock in Jersey City, New Jersey.

The only place in the United States to see a "moonbow"—a kind of rainbow you can see at night—is at Cumberland Falls, Kentucky.

The highest tides in the United States are in Passamaquoddy Bay in Maine.

More breakfast cereal is made in Battle Creek, Michigan, than in any other city in the world.

The world's tallest and fastest roller coaster is in California.

The Mississippi River is the longest river in the United States.

Lake Superior is the largest lake in the United States.

Mount McKinley, in Alaska, is the highest mountain in the United States.

More Fabulous Facts

The biggest man-made hole in the world is an open-pit iron mine in Minnesota. It is almost 4 miles (almost 6½ kilometers) long, almost 2 miles (more than 3 kilometers) wide, and almost 500 feet (almost 150 meters) deep.

Montana has about 3 head of cattle for every person in the state.

The largest underground lake in the U.S. is the Lost Sea in Craighead Cavern, in Tennessee.

The world's largest fossil of a mammoth—13 feet 4½ inches (4 meters) high—was found in Nebraska.

Death Valley is 282 feet (85 meters) below sea level. It is the lowest place in the United States.

New Hampshire has the shortest ocean coastline of any state. It is only 13 miles (21 kilometers) long.

Point Barrow, Alaska, is the most northern spot in the United States.

Alaska has a longer coastline than all the other 49 states put together. It is 6,640 miles (10,624 kilometers) long.

The sun shines 20 hours a day during the summer in Alaska.

The only place in the United States where four states come together is at Four Corners. That's where Arizona, Colorado, New Mexico, and Utah meet.

Bagdad, in Death Valley, California, had no rain for over two years — 760 days — from October 3, 1912, to November 8, 1914.

The marble used to build the Tomb of the Unknown Soldier in Arlington, Virginia, was mined in Marble, Colorado.

The world's highest suspension bridge goes across Royal Gorge in Colorado. It is 1,053 feet (316 meters) above the floor of the gorge.

Maine makes more wooden toothpicks than any other state — about 100 million a day.

More Fabulous Facts

The strongest wind ever measured blew 231 miles (370 kilometers) per hour on the top of Mount Washington in New Hampshire in 1934.

 The National Marbles Tournament is held in June each year at Wildwood, New Jersey.

The first night baseball game was played in Cincinnati, Ohio, in 1935.

California grows more food than any other state.

The smallest state has the longest name — State of Rhode Island and Providence Plantations.

The first printing press used in the United States can now be seen in Montpelier, Vermont.

The first United States Mint was in Pennsylvania.